Adam Millard is the author of seventeen novellas, and more than two hundred short stories, which can be found in various collections and anthologies. Probably best known for his post-apocalyptic fiction, Adam also writes fantasy/horror for children, as well as bizarro fiction for several publishers. His work has been translated for the German, Spanish, and Russian markets. He lives in Newcastle-under-Lyme with his wife, Dawn, and his two cats, Butter and Toast.

Copyright 2024 Adam Millard
This Edition Published 2024 by Crowded Quarantine Publications
The moral right of the author has been asserted
All characters in this publication are fictitious and any resemblance to real persons, living or dead, is purely coincidental.

All rights reserved.
No part of this publication may be reproduced, stored in a retrieval system, or transmitted, in any form or by any means without the prior permission in writing of the publisher, nor be otherwise circulated in any form of binding or cover other than that in which it is published and without a similar condition including this condition being imposed on the subsequent purchase.
A CIP catalogue record for this book is available from the British Library

ISBN: 978-1-7384764-9-7

Crowded Quarantine Publications
124 Dimsdale Parade West
Newcastle-Under-Lyme. Staffordshire
ST5 8DU

BABY RUDOLPH

ADAM MILLARD

1

Finklefoot stared incredulously at the fork sticking from the back of Shart's hand as if it were an alien, recently exploded from an unfortunate human's chest. Blood pooled around the tines, fifty percent of which were embedded in the stupid elf's hand. A quick glance up from the carnage, to Shart's ridiculous face and the nonchalant expression he currently affected, told Finklefoot everything he needed to know about Shart: he was a fucking idiot.

"So that's it, is it?" Finklefoot asked of his cohort. "At this year's Land of Christmas Annual Variety Show, you have eschewed the usual fare, decided not to sing something nice in the classic *bel canto* styling, or furnish the audience with a well-choreographed street-dance, nor even pull a baby seal out of a hat where there most certainly had not been one before." He took a quick slug of his ale; his mouth was drier than a popcorn fart. "Instead of those things," he continued, setting his tankard back down on the bar, "you are going to stick a fork in your hand and pretend it doesn't hurt?"

BABY RUDOLPH

"Correct," Shart whimpered, eyes still bulging, and he took to wiping frantically at the pooling blood with the back of his mitten. "I'll tell you something, though," he said. "The bleeding stops after about an hour or so, but it don't half hurt for *days* after."

Finklefoot yanked the fork from Shart's bloody hand and threw it across the counter. It was noisy—it veritably clattered as it went—and the other patrons of THE PARTRIDGE INN (*a pear tree!*) turned to see what the hubbub was. "You, sir," he said, "are an absolute moron."

"No," Shart said, pulling his mitten back on and concealing the offending wound. "It won't just be my *hand*. I can do my leg, or my arse, or my—"

"I'd rather you didn't say it," Finklefoot interrupted, just in the nick of time. "And please, pull your trousers back up, before you get us both barred." So, not quite in the nick of time.

Shart pulled his trousers up and buckled his belt. "So, you see?" he said. "It's not as if I'm a one-trick pony."

"A pony," Finklefoot said, still averting his gaze, "you most certainly are not." He waited a moment, saw that everything had been tucked away once more, and continued. "You really can't expect to win the Land of Christmas

Annual Variety Show by just sticking forks in bits of yourself and pretending it doesn't hurt. There's no *skill* to it, Shart. *Anyone* can do that."

"Then why *don't* they?" countered Shart, without an ounce of irony. For a moment, Finklefoot was suitably flummoxed. Fortunately, the need for a response was removed with the most-welcome arrival of the barman, Norm.

"Why is there a puddle of blood on my bar?" Norm asked, pointing at same with a well-chewed pencil. To Shart he said, "You've not learnt your lesson from last week, have you?"

Shart, who had turned a whiter shade of pale, clutched onto the bar to steady himself. "I was just showing Finklefoot," he said, "what I was doing at the variety show. I won't do it again." He put his head down on the counter, fainting dead away from blood-loss.

Norm rolled his eyes; Finklefoot rolled two coins in the barman's direction. "Same again please, Norm."

As the barman set about pouring a pint of 'same again' into Finklefoot's special tankard, he glanced about the place and did shakings of his head and tuttings of his tongue. He also did furtive fartings from the back-passage and burpings from the front, but the less said about that the better. Sensing what Norm was referring to with his head-shaking and tutting, Finklefoot said:

"It's a bit quiet in here tonight, Norm."

Norm sighed and pushed the tankard of 'same again' toward his favourite barfly. "They're all at home, I imagine, practising dance moves and swallowing giant candy-canes." He lit his miniature corncob pipe and filled the space around him with gingerbread smoke.

"Not into it all then?" Finklefoot said, "The Land of Christmas Annual Variety Show?"

"What's not to like?" Norm replied, sarcastically. "It makes for great entertainment, it does. Who doesn't want to see Gizzo the Great deepthroating a candy-cane, or Shart here stabbing himself almost to death with kitchen cutlery? I mean, *Live at the Apollo* must be shitting itself."

Finklefoot snorted. "Sarcasm duly noted," he said.

"Hey, you're not getting involved in all this variety show nonsense, are you?" asked Norm.

"I'm a respected foreman of the toy factory," Finklefoot reminded him, for he was. "You think I've got time for all that malarkey?"

Norm didn't, and was about to say as much when Finklefoot cut him off.

"Not me, Norm," he said, "I've got rotas to schedule, chitties to sign, toys to check, elves to sack, spreadsheets to stare at with confusion, elves to hire, warehouses to fill, materials to acquire, bills to pay, lights to keep on, children to make happy, elves to sack..." He trailed off there, for he had surely covered the salient points. "In other words," he added, "fuck the fucking variety show."

"That's what I like to hear," Norm said. "Stick it to the man!" Whatever the hell that meant.

"Same again," Finklefoot said, for he had emptied another tankard. All this talk of the Land of Christmas Annual Variety Show had lit a spark within Finklefoot. He was slightly enraged—an oxymoron, if ever there was one—and everyone knows that angry drinkers drink quicker. There's no rhyme or reason to it, it's just one of those things. Angry drinkers drink quicker, sleepy drivers crash more, horny bastards fuck harder, and so on and so forth.

It was then, as Finklefoot considered the almost preternatural might of amorous elves, that two of his hardest-working labourers made an entrance.

BABY RUDOLPH

Rat and Jimbo paused as they entered, perhaps expecting an applause or a cheer as if this were some 1980s human sitcom, and when none was forthcoming, they continued to the bar.

"Evening, boss," Jimbo offered, pulling up a stool alongside Finklefoot and jumping up onto it. "I've just squashed my bollocks," he said through gritted teeth.

"Jimbo," Finklefoot said, for it was only right he should acknowledge the presence of one of his most loyal lackeys.

"Evening, boss," Rat said, leaning against the bar on the other side of Finklefoot.

"Yes, quite," said the foreman. "Look, is this some sort of hostage situation?" He waved a hand frantically from one elf to the other. "You're flanking me, and I don't like to be flanked, not without kissing me first. And you," he said to Rat, "are close enough to warrant one or both of us taking a pregnancy test as soon as possible."

Rat's bottom half took a step back but everything above the waist remained in place. "Sorry, boss," he said. "Can I buy you a drink?"

"No thank you, Rat," Finklefoot said, and then, "Hang on, you've never bought me a drink, not once, ever, in this history of you, I, and ale, never have you put your mittens into your overalls and paid for a drink for anyone other than yourself."

"Feeling generous," said Rat, drawing his sleeve along his nostrils and leaving a snail trail that would glisten beneath the phosphorous lights for the remainder of the evening.

"You're *after* something," Finklefoot quickly realised. "You want something from me, and I'm likely to say no, so you're trying to butter me up with ale, paid for from your own pocket." He took a breath before adding, "You can fuck off."

"Charming, that is," said Rat.

"That's a little bit harsh," Jimbo added from the other side. Finklefoot had almost forgotten about him. As, one might imagine, did many of you. "He was only offering you a pint of 'same again',"

"No strings attached," said Rat, holding his hands out as if to prove they were empty of anything offensive or dodgy.

"Three pints of 'same again', is it?" asked Norm.

"How can we have 'same again'?" Jimbo asked with a frown. "We haven't had *anything* yet."

"Yeah, we haven't had *anything* yet," Rat said, pointing at the space in front of him where there should, by now, be a pint of something. *Anything.*

BABY RUDOLPH

"Two pints of anything coming right up," Norm said, and he set about pouring them.

"And a pint of 'same again' for Finklefoot, when he's ready," Rat insisted. Finklefoot had all but given up on refusing; the sonsofbitches were going to get their way, whatever happened. It was best just to hear them out, say no, and then move forward from there.

"Okay," Finklefoot said, when the silence became too deafening to stand. "What is it you're after?"

Rat looked at Jimbo.

Jimbo looked at Rat.

Finklefoot looked at them both, and when neither spoke, he said, "Well, that was fascinating. I shall just finish my 'same again' in peace, and you two can stare wistfully into each other's faces."

"We need a third," Rat said, suddenly. Jimbo's eyes widened, as if he couldn't quite believe his friend had spoken.

Finklefoot was confused, and his expression said as much. You could park a car between those frown lines. "A third what?" he said. "A third lunch-break? A third Sunday shift? A third bollock?"

"A third *elf*," Jimbo said, joining the conversation, if only to steer it in the right direction momentarily. "You see, there has to be *three* of us, and so far there's only Rat and me."

"No there isn't," Finklefoot said, and he performed a headcount. "One, two, three," he said. "There are three of us already. Four if you count Norm."

"Don't count on me for *anything*," said the barman, collecting coins from Rat. "I'm barely even here, and probably won't be for long periods of the plot." With that, he turned and walked through a door that might have led to somewhere else but was probably just a cupboard.

"Oh!" Finklefoot said. "Well, now there *are* just three of us, which is perfect, Rat, Jimbo, because that's how many you wanted in the first place."

Rat sipped furtively at his ale; a froth moustache immediately replaced his real one, but both were white and fluffy, so no one really noticed. In fact, if it hadn't been brought up at all—

"While you are correct that there are indeed three of us," Jimbo said, "you are apparently missing the point. We need three elves to do a certain thing, and we are currently one short."

"We are all three short," Finklefoot said, for height jokes never went out of fashion, especially when you were an elf amongst elves.

"What he's trying to say," Rat said, "is that we need you, boss, to complete our threesome."

Finklefoot grunted, for he was thoroughly annoyed now. "I beg your pardon?" he said. "I'm not into all that... that sexy nonsense, and..." he turned to face Jimbo, "you should be ashamed of yourself. You're *married*, Jimbo! Have been for centuries! Does Sissy know about this?" He thought for a second before returning again with more vigour. "*I'm* married! Does *my* wife know about this? You sicken me, both of you!"

"I was already gonna throw up," said Shart, lifting his head up from the bar long enough to get through his lines. "But you three sickos have made it worse." He went back to sleep.

"Not *that* sort of threesome!" Jimbo said, perishing the thought. "Although I have heard they *can* be fun, depending on which of you gets the good end."

Finklefoot frowned. "Wasn't that the main plot of the last book?"

They all shrugged.

"No, we're looking for a third elf, boss, and we want you to be it." Jimbo said.

"A third elf for *what*!" said Finklefoot, exasperated.

"Our *Bee Gees* tribute band for the Land of Christmas Annual Variety Show!" Rat excitedly said.

Finklefoot nodded, affected a fake smile, and said:

"Fuck off."

BABY RUDOLPH

2

In The Land of Christmas, no matter the time of year, two things are guaranteed. The first thing is that Christmas is always just around the corner, no matter whether it is January, June, or November. Elves work three-hundred-and-sixty-five days a year, and an extra day on Leap years, to ensure that everything is just so, and that Christmas goes ahead without a hitch. It is an elf's only true purpose in life, and to not take up work placement in any one of the many factories—the liquorice factory, the jigsaw house, tin robot depot, battery quarter (where, by law, every third box packed must be without batteries), dolls and stuffed toys, etc.—is considered a federal offence, punishable by exile to Earth, where a convict's remaining days will be spent as one of seven in a shitty pantomime or as a heavily made-up goblin or dwarf in Hollywood feature films. The most common example of this is Warwick Davis, whose real name is Wizzle, and who was banished after trying to unionise the Matchbox car factory. As bedtime stories, parents recount Wizzle's life in the form of terrifying psalms and haunting nursery rhymes, and it serves to keep them on the straight and narrow, albeit with dirty sheets and, later on, spiralling therapy bills.

The second guarantee in The Land of Christmas is snow. Snow. Snow. Snow. And when it isn't snowing—which it is, always—it is sleeting. Great big sheets of it coming down all the time, so much snow they don't know what to do with it, and so they don't do anything anymore. Underfloor heating was installed at some point in history, which melts the snow closest to the ground more quickly, but more snow still comes, and so, as some sort of inclement winter wonderland perpetual motion machine, it goes on and on and on, ad nauseum.

Snow.

So, it goes without saying—which I have, at great detail anyway, it seems—that it was currently snowing bucket-loads in the streets and all about and around. Imagine, if you will, a merry village, all multicoloured lights strung from post-to-post and Christmas music hanging in the air like a Sunday dinner fart. We are at some distance now, above the streets, looking down upon the scenery with jaws agape and hearts racing. It is a tableau of Christmas perfection; one that could be painted and printed and slapped on the front of a Christmas card to give to your granny for, hopefully, what would be the last time, as cards aren't getting any cheaper, and she ain't getting any younger.

Now, imagine as we slowly push in and the scenery comes closer, and the music becomes ever-so-slightly louder, and we swoop low along the pure-white snow through the streets, through the legs of a delivery elf as he's making his rounds, and past the decadent bakery on the corner, which makes those wonderful gingerbread people with or without cocks (it doesn't matter! It's gingerbread!) and we swing a left at the village's Herculean Christmas tree and arrive at our destination.

A small window, just above pavement level, which means almost wholly covered over with snow, except for perhaps an inch in which we can squeeze through if we breathe in, and so we do, and now we're in, and, well, what the fuck do we do now? It would probably be best to revert to conventional storytelling techniques.

Yes, that would be for the best.

The basement was dark. Not so dark as to hide things, but dark enough to not be able to see much at all. Put another way, you wouldn't want to be caught in it halfway through a crossword puzzle.

Ahora sighed. She sighed a lot these days, as would you if you had been plucked from an alleyway in the dead of night, chloroformed to within an inch of her life, and elf-handled into a basement somewhere or other, and subsequently a cage no bigger than her lavatory at home. Sighing was one of the only things she had left now that her voice had gone; lost from the endless hours of screaming and shouting for help. Yes, Ahora's lot was not a happy one.

Oh, and it was made worse still by the strange and unmistakeable stench of shit and piss constantly permeating the air, not all of which was her own. At least, she hoped it wasn't, for it veritably stank, and she'd never had herself down as a stinker. Positively lady elf-like, Ahora was, with bum-toots smelling of roses and suchlike.

Suddenly, light spilled into the room, not quite reaching Ahora's cell—for that's what it was—but enough to cast a yellow oblong along the floor of the basement. Then came the footsteps as her captor descended the basement steps, and the gentle tinkle of fine crockery as its carrier came down.

"You will eat this, Ahora," said the voice, which now appeared as a shadow, stretched out across the entire length of the basement floor. A shadow which grew shorter and shorter, and then became a figure, stood in front of the cell door holding a tray, upon which sat a soup bowl and a glass of water with a solitary rose in it.

"I'm not hungry," Ahora lied as she pushed herself up into a sitting position. Her voice was croaky, her throat sorer than an alter boy's backside. "And how do I know it's not poisoned?"

Her elfnapper laughed a little at this; it sounded like an old car trying to start on a cold, winter's morning. Horrible sound, it was. "I'm not going to kill you," said her captor as she opened the small door at the bottom of the cage and slowly pushed the tray through. "I'd have thought you'd figured that out by now."

Ahora sighed once more. "Just let me go," she whispered. "Please, just let—"

The door at the bottom of the cage slammed shut and was locked up nice and tight once again. As the figure made its way across the basement, it said, "Make sure to eat it all up. Otherwise, you'll starve yourself to death, and that's just not on, is it?"

And then they were gone, and semi-darkness once more fell across the basement. Ahora sobbed, for she was utterly lost, and prayed, for she was one of *those* sorts of elves. Five minutes passed, and when she could cry no more tears, she tucked into the soup, and rather nice it was, too, for a minestrone.

BABY RUDOLPH

3

Morning, once again, and snow, as fucking always. The outdoor rinks were a hive of activity as the reindeer groups gathered in their herds, preparatory to the day's intense training schedule.

On Rink One, a Zamboni® went round and round, getting it ready for its first hooves of the morning. You couldn't have a rink full of divots and snow-bumps, and certainly not on Rink One, which was where Santa's Eight trained and perfected their take-offs and landings. Sure, no one would notice a little hole here or there on Rinks Two and Three, or a build-up of snow on Rink Four (which happened more often than the Rink Caretaker liked to admit) but Rink One was always immaculate. Think of it like the centre-court of Wimbledon; perfectly-tended grass, beautifully green and chalk markings bright and sharp. Now dump a foot of snow on top of it, and you're not far shy of the mark.

The other rinks were like Wimbledon's other courts. Sure, they were fit for purpose, but no one, not really, if they were being honest with themselves, wanted to train or play on them, and even the groundskeepers didn't give a shit, which is why those secondary courts always look like your nan's backyard.

Playing order of the day, as it were, on Rink One was take-offs, followed by black-ice emergency stops, and then after lunch three hours of landings and turbulence practise. Quite often there would be exercises thrown in at the last minute, such as bird collision techniques and how to avoid them, and recent addition to the syllabus, onshore windfarms and subsequent first aid applications.

The great reindeer Odin would be supervising the morning's training on Rink One, with Thor taking over after lunch, as Odin had a vet appointment he just couldn't get out of.

The Eight were currently warming up, waiting for the Zamboni® to finish doing its things, and generally talking amongst themselves when Rudolph sidled up to the group, stretching his legs this way and that, and rolling his neck about the place, as one always does before a day of intense schooling.

"So," Rudolph said, in that way people often do when they're trying to fit in. "What do reindeers want for Christmas?" He was already smiling, because this one was a cracker. At least he thought so.

BABY RUDOLPH

Vixen wrapped a band around her head, spat on the snow in front of Rudolph, and said, in no uncertain terms, "Go fuck yourself."

It would have been quite a shocking display, had not we all heard of the terrible bullying poor Rudolph had to put up with. It was simply accepted that he should be treated with such contempt, which didn't make it right, of course, just... well, what good would the song be if he *didn't*, occasionally, get it in the neck, hm?

The cocky little cunt.

"No, you're going to like this one," Rudolph went on. Like water off a duck's back, it was. "What do all reindeers want for Christmas?" With more fervency now, too, as if he couldn't wait to get to the punchline.

"The day off!" Blitzen said. "But that ain't gonna happen, is it, because the Fat Bastard won't let us get fair pay, for a fair day's work, and—"

"Don't get yourself all wound up again," said Donner, patting Blitzen upon the back with a snow-covered hoof. "The Fat Bastard doesn't lose any sleep over you, now, does he, so let's just do our jobs, get paid, and get home to our wives and kids, yeah?"

"Easy for you to say," said Blitzen. "I had to eat my kids last winter, Dark days, these are, when there's not enough money to put food that isn't your own children on the table."

"What do all reindeers want for Christmas!?" Rudolph said, completely not reading the room.

"Oh, just piss of with your jokes, Rudy," Prancer said. "They're never funny, and the way you tell them doesn't help."

"You have," said Dasher, "the delivery skills of an epileptic midwife, Rudy. Jokes aren't your thing. Stick to something you're good at, like..." There was a long pause as all eight, nine if you counted the subject, tried to produce something Rudolph *was* good at.

"Look, just accept it, man," said Blitzen. "You're never going to make it as a stand-up comedian. And if you're thinking of entering the Land of Christmas Annual Variety Show with *your* jokes, then you've got more balls than I, and a helluva lot thicker skin, because they're just going to laugh at you."

"That's the point!" said Rudolph, missing the point. "I want them to laugh at me! My jokes are brilliant. I know it, and so will they once they figure them out. I'm a thinking man's comic, like Stewart Lee or Bill Hicks."

BABY RUDOLPH

"You're a Peter Kay, at best," said Vixen.

"A pony sleigh-station!" Rudolph said, which made extraordinarily little sense in the context of things.

"What?" Prancer asked, hoping to clear things up.

"That's what all reindeers want for Christmas!" Rudolph said, a huge smile stretching across his phizzog, as if he was proud of it. "A pony sleigh-station!"

"I don't..."

"Hm?"

"Fuck off, red-nosed prick..."

"I... what?"

"... don't get it."

"Oh."

The consensus, it seemed, was that the joke was a little too intellectual for them, perhaps relying somewhat heavily upon the wordplay element, rather than the overall sum of its parts. Then there was, of course, the slight chance they were not well-versed in the names and history of earthly video-games consoles, and therefore—

"That was fucking shite, mate," Blitzen said, and spat in Rudolph's eye. "It might have worked if we were ponies, lad, but we're reindeer."

Like a sex-doll in a house fire, Rudolph visibly deflated. It had been his opener, the gag which he'd planned to kick off his set with, and it didn't do well to fall at the first hurdle. *Never mind*, Rudolph thought. Just a quick shuffle here and there, and he'd put the joke a little further along, once he had the audience on his side and eating out of his hoof, so to speak.

"I thought it was hilarious," a voice said.

It wasn't one of those disembodied voices which sometimes come during the night, when the stable's all creepy and everyone else is asleep. It was a gentle, almost ethereal voice. Rather lovely, it was, and it came from behind, and so Rudolph quickly took to turning to see who the delightful voice belonged to.

"Gah!" Rudolph said, for the voice most certainly did not match the curtains, or suchlike. A veritable heifer of a reindeer was marching toward him; her head bobbed up and down with every heavy step she took. The ground didn't shake, as it might during an ice quake, however Rudolph felt it just the same, and his fillings did febrile rattlings in his mouth.

"Oh my!" said the cow, which had never been more apt a description for a female reindeer. "Oh my, he's looking at me!

BABY RUDOLPH

Rudolph is looking at me!" And she set about fluttering her eyelashes, of which there seemed to be more than usual. Even her antlers were fat, if such a thing were possible.

Affecting nervousness—and also fear—Rudolph said, "Oh, my... um, please don't hurt me."

The newcomer smiled; a half-chewed carrot fell from somewhere within her face and thumped into the snow between them. "Don't be silly, little Rudy," she said, and Rudolph caught a whiff of her breath, and oh, Lord of all that is good and pure, did he turn his head so that he should not have the displeasure of catching another breath full-face. "I'm a big fan of yours," she went on. "Have been since you first used your nose, you clever little so-and-so. Oh, to be in the presence of greatness, it doesn't half make one wet in the nethers, yes indeed!"

To that, Rudolph did not know what to say, for his mother had taught him to be polite and never engage someone in conversation if their main subject is about their genitalia, and the dampness thereof. Very nice woman, Rudolph's mother. Shame she was killed by poachers, really.

"You're hilarious, Rudy!" the cow went on. "I've heard you telling jokes before, and they always make me laugh, so they do." She paused to undo the top button of her pink cardigan, though quite what that was all about, Rudolph hadn't the foggiest. "What's the one about..." And here she took to impersonating Rudolph in what could only be described as, for want of a better thesaurus, an uncannily accurate fashion. "What do reindeers use to communicate?"

Rudolph knew the answer. Of course he fucking did, it was his joke. "The antlernet," he said, somewhat self-consciously, for that impression had all but done for him the way Alec Baldwin did for Trump.

"The antlernet!" said the cow, and her eyes filled up with tears and she struggled for breath for what seemed like an eternity, as laughter completely took her over. And also, some shit fell out the back of her.

It was a good joke, Rudolph thought, but not that good, which meant this woman was either very easily tickled—which, judging by the size of her, was not on option, for her funny bone was in there somewhere, buried beneath twenty inches of blubbery reindeer meat, and wholly untouchable without the use of a power-drill and a two-foot drill-bit—or she was mocking him. Taking the piss, the same way Prancer and Blitzen and all the others did.

Finally, and not a moment too soon, the female deer ceased her laughter, and once more became stoic. A little *too* stoic, for Rudolph's liking. She looked like a veritable madwoman as she quickly tidied her perm, which had fallen out of place during the uncontrollable laughter.

"Oh, Rudy!" she said, her rancid breath almost reaching Rudolph, who took a furtive step back to in a quiet effort to avoid it. "Are you training today?" This line came out so sombrely, it might as well have been delivered by a robot.

"Yeah, I'm on Rink Two in about ten minutes," he said, almost immediately regretting it. Something about this portly cow fairly put the shits up him, and yet there was no real reason for it. She seemed amiable enough, and her laughter was, although hellishly pungent, somewhat addictive, but there was something not quite right about her that Rudolph couldn't quite put his dewclaw on. "You here to spectate, are you?" he asked.

At this she snorted, and it was not a nice snort. It was the kind of snort one might expect to receive if one had just passed wind in an overcrowded elevator.

"I'm actually *flying* on Rink Four," she said, emphasis on the 'flying', which immediately caused Rudolph to feel bad, for he had assumed, what with her being almost twice the regulation-size for a flier, that she would be better off keeping her hooves firmly attached to the ground, where she could cause no real damage, other than to her own heart. "I'm working my way up through the ranks," she said, "and one day, one day... you mark my words, Rudy, the name Merthyr Titful will be on everyone's lips."

"Is that your name then, is it?" Rudolph said. "Is that what we're going for in this touching, powerful, and extremely sensitive plot? Merthyr Titful?"

The cow, Merthyr, did noddings of the oversized head and exhaled plumes of smelly air through her nose, which immediately turned to fog in the cold. "Merthyr," she said, holding out a hoof. "And it's an absolute pleasure to meet you, Rudy," said she.

Rudolph cautiously bumped hooves with Merthyr, watching as her face lit up like a Halloween jack-o-lantern and trying to figure out just what it was about her that set him on edge, other than the obvious.

"Well," Rudolph said, putting his hoof back down and backing slowly away. "Good luck with your, ahem, flying, Merthyr," he said, almost bumping into Vixen, who was doing short sprints behind him.

Merthyr waved, which was a fucking ridiculous thing to be doing, since they were still within spitting distance of one another, and her face affected something like utter joy, as if an item had just been ticked off on her bucket list and she could now move onto the next thing.

"See you around, Rudy!" she said, and then she leaned back onto her haunches, planted her not inconsiderable backside in the snow, and took a massive piss, which pooled out in all directions, a great yellow stream that melted everything in its path, and Rudolph, who had been unable to take his eyes off the cow, now did so, for his mother had also taught him never to watch while another deer slashes, which was good of her.

Rudolph headed over to Rink Two, tripping and struggling through the snow, his main motor functions seemingly affected by his unhinged encounter with a certain Merthyr Titful.

And Merthyr, she watched him go with many lickings of the lips and strokings of things that are better left up to the imagination, and even then, I wouldn't recommend it.

4

Now here is something you *can* imagine, if it's your predilection, without feeling wholly unsettled and more than a little bilious about. A tissue, however, might come in handy, lest one's handy become filled with come. Or something.

The woman, for she was certainly one of those, slid purposefully up and down the titanium-gold pole, and she threw legs all around and about, which sounds like she might have more than the regulation two, and it certainly appeared that way as they wrapped themselves around the pole and then kicked out and somersaulted up it in contradiction to all known laws of gravity. She smoothly gyrated against the cold titanium-gold, her satin red knickers, pleated with white faux fur about the leg-holes and waist, rubbing up and down and generally making squeaking noises.

"Is that necessary, Jessica?" said The Fat Bastard from behind his cluttered desk. "It's very hard to concentrate with you, whirling round that pole like a dervish."

As if the dollar-bill had been unceremoniously ripped from the waistband of her knickers, Jessica Claus stopped gyrating and slid down the pole the way a bird-shit might slide down the windshield of a Ford Cortina. In other words, there was very little sexy about it.

Santa, aka Father Christmas, aka Old Saint Nick, aka The Fat Bastard, worked through the stacks of paper on his desk, moving them this way and that, trying to locate something that either simply wasn't there, or was playing funny buggers and hiding.

"Lost something, dear?" Jessica asked as she pulled herself into a tight bra and took to fastening it in that clever way that only women know how.

"Last year's tax returns," said The Fat Bastard, taking up a stapler and setting it back down again in another place. "I swear, things are being moved around by someone without my knowledge, and it fairly pisses me—" He stopped there, snatched up a document from his desk, and said, "Never mind. I've found them. As you were. Up and down the pole you go, dear, whatever makes you happy."

Jessica Claus huffed silently at this, for the only thing that truly made her happy these days were her secret rendezvous with several of the worker elves, who shall remain unnamed to avoid litigation. Also, there were more than just several. Numerous might be more apt; plus, it sounded far better than, *She'll fuck anything that moves as long as it's shorter than three feet.*

"I'm all danced out for one day," yawned Jessica, and now she was robed in the standard-issue red-and-white cotton affair with the occasionally twinkling fairy-light waist tie. It looked far better on her than it did The Fat Bastard.

"Yes, well," said Santa, "I've got rather a lot to be getting on with here, I'm afraid. If you're looking for something to do, there is an office party going on over in Finance that might benefit from your presence."

Jessica's ears perked up at this, which is extraordinary to see when it happens, as ears are far more suited to the perked-down position. "Finance?" she said, dreamily. "All those male elves, half-drunk on egg-nog and cheap champagne, no doubt celebrating another successful quarter and just counting down the hours to the end of the day so that they might return home to their wives and give it to them good and proper in further celebration?"

"I should imagine that's how it goes, dear," said The Fat Bastard not taking his eyes off the document in front of him. "Horny, drunk elves, quite indeed, my dear," he added.

Jessica Claus did not need telling twice; she seldom needed telling *once*, and quickly pecked her husband tenderly upon the cheek before making good her exit before he realised what he had just sent his wife into and changed his mind.

The Fat Bastard, suddenly all alone in his office—just the way he liked it, which begged the question of why he had had that pole installed in the first place; the view, probably, or maybe because he liked the smell—took out a bottle of Scotch and poured himself a large one.

Just then, the phone rang, as it was wont to do upon occasion, and he answered with a, "What the fuck is it now?" as if it were a common occurrence, when in fact that particular telephone hadn't made a peep in almost half a decade.

"Mr. Claus?" said a tiny, high-pitched voice.

The Fat Bastard winced. Elf voices really wound him up; it wasn't conducive to his role as King of the Land of Christmas, but if you've never had to listen to a whiny elf going on and on about all and sundry, then you were, Santa opined, extremely fortunate.

"Yes, yes, what is it?" he huffed, for he had a thousand things to be going on with, and answering the phone first thing of a Monday morning was not one of them.

"My name is Twot, sir," said the voice, "and I'm a worker at the jigsaw factory."

"How wonderful for you, Twot," said The Fat Bastard. "But if it's a raise you're looking for, you'll have to speak with Ahora. She's the forelady down there, and—"

"Well, that's just the thing, sir," said Twot, who was removing his little pointy hat and scratching at his head and wiping snow from his shoulders, all things that The Fat Bastard couldn't see due to this being a phone call. "Ahora isn't here."

Santa almost choked on a mouthful of Scotch as it went down the wrong way. "What?" he said. "What do you mean she's not there? Of course she's there! It's a Monday morning, a new week, a fresh start, and she's the forelady, and has the only set of keys to get into the factory, therefore she must be there, otherwise..." And The Fat Bastard trailed off there as chaotic images ran through his head. Pictures of a mile-long queue, snaking all the way round the factory building; shivering elves all covered with snow, the shorter ones blanketed entirely; inside the factory, machines lying dormant, unused, silent, off.

"Are you still there, sir?" enquired Twot.

BABY RUDOLPH

"Of *course* I'm still here," grunted The Fat Bastard, and he slammed a heavy fist down on the desk, displacing a decade's worth of dust and shed skin. "Now, you listen to me and you listen well," he went on. "I'm putting you in charge until this whole thing is sorted out."

Twot tried to interject, to refuse the position entirely, but there simply wasn't time.

"Do you hear me, Twot?"

"Ye—"

"Now, I assume you've already checked for a spare key to the factory."

"Why would you assume that, sir?"

"Well, it makes sense, doesn't it? Are you at the main entrance now?"

"Yes, sir."

"And do you see perhaps a doormat under which a spare key might be located? Perhaps a flowerpot? One of those ridiculous plastic stones with the false arse? Get with me on this, Twot, or begone!"

"There's nothing like that, sir," said Twot, who was now crying a little. The Fat Bastard could hear his muffled sobs on the other end.

"Have you tried kicking the door in?" said Santa. "Take a run up, and put your foot right through the blasted thing?"

"We tried using Blip as a battering ram, sir, but it just pushed his head into his body. I'm afraid that, not only did the door refuse to budge, but it now has a rather unsightly dent in it. Blip's not in a good way, neither."

The Fat Bastard nodded; at least they were being proactive about it, which was something.

"Okay! All right! Don't panic, Twot!" said Santa. "I shall have this all sorted before lunchtime. Tell the workforce to go home, but also tell them that they're on call and that this is not, under any circumstances, a day off. All being well I'll have that factory up and running before your lot have a chance to get comfortable."

"Yes, sir," Twot said, and then added, "But what about Ahora, sir? It's hardly like her to be not showing up for work, sir, and I'm worried that something terrible might have happened to her, sir. What if she's fallen down the stairs, or come down with the Covid, sir?"

The Fat Bastard fairly grimaced at the mention of Covid; that terrible exordium to the End Times whose reign of terror had all but cancelled two Christmases and put a third on short notice. What an appalling time that had been, and it wasn't over yet, for there were still signs of it about the place. Even in The Land of Christmas, elves of a particular mindset continued to wear their N95s; hand sanitiser was still regularly utilised, and a fair number of elves were still regularly hospitalised as a result, not of Covid, but from drinking all the bleach.

"I very much doubt," said The Fat Bastard, "that anything terrible has happened to Ahora. I will set about finding her post-haste so that you and your colleagues can get back to doing what you do best. Cutting images of cats and dogs and landscape paintings into intricate little pieces to frustrate the elderly of Earth."

And, with that, he hung up.

Twot pushed his tongue into his bottom lip—the universal sign for 'my, you are a silly sausage, aren't you?'—and did furtive jabbings at the phone with two fingers—the universal sign for 'fuck off, you absolute knob of a tool!'—before passing on the update to his colleagues.

Of course, Santa saw none of this because he wasn't there.

"Oh, deary me," said The Fat Bastard, for his week was off to a terrible start, and it wasn't even ten o'clock!

He poured another large Scotch, stood, and belched deeply, and walked across the room, where he sniffed the titanium-gold pole as if it were a liquorice lace.

"Righty ho-ho-ho," said he, returning to his desk feeling somewhat better. "Let's find this bitch before all Hell breaks loose."

BABY RUDOLPH

5

The morning's flight training went about as well as possible, with very few in the way of injuries and even fewer in the way of deaths (poor Thunder! Santa rest his soul).

Rudolph, satisfied with a few things, but not his overall landing score, trotted across to the troughs at the far end of Rink Two, away from everyone, so that he might eat in peace and work on a few new jokes, if time allowed before the afternoon session.

He ate, lichen and fungi, willow and birch, and once full, he took a notepad and pen from his training bag and took to a quiet bench at the side of the stable.

Now, there are questions to be asked regarding a reindeer's ability to write, what with all the hoofage and dewclaws, but needless to say that sometimes, a suspension of disbelief comes in handy. Rudolph could write just fine. Sure, it was a little bit scruffy, like that of an inebriated General Practitioner, but it was legible to him, and that was enough.

Flipping open the notebook, he quickly ran through the jokes presently therein, chortling to himself, for he was indeed the veritable exemplar of a funny fucker, and soon everyone would know it.

Happy with his work thus far, he set to scrawling more humorous one-liners and titillating anecdotes. There was a bit about his childhood, a gag about his dead mother—for dark humour was not beyond this particular reindeer, and so help anyone that judged him for it—and then a series of paronomastic jokes that would hopefully have them rolling in the aisles, choking on their scratchings and coughing up ale and egg-nog like there was no tomorrow. He was particularly proud of a bit involving props, in which he transformed himself into the current president of the United States of America and proceeded to urinate over a coconut shaped like Vladimir Putin, and if that didn't work, he thought, then nothing would.

Rudolph was in the process of coming up with a suitable punchline to, *What do you call a reindeer on Halloween?* when he noticed the nearby sound of slurping and chewing.

Horrible, it was, and when Rudolph looked up from his notes and saw Merthyr Titful, grazing from the trough and getting it all over and around her fat face and pink cardigan, he tried to make himself smaller so as not to be discovered there, nestled away in the corner.

BABY RUDOLPH

"Writing, are you?" Merthyr said without turning, and also without a hint of mirth. Rudolph didn't know what was more frightening, the impassive tone of her voice or the massive arse and vagina he could see between swingings of an overweight tail.

"Um, just... yeah," said Rudolph. He felt cornered. In fact, he *was* cornered. He was the very description of cornered. If you were to look 'cornered' up in a dictionary, there he would be, a picture of him sitting on that bench with the look of a buggered man about his face. Followed by the synonyms: entrapped, enclosed, penned in, and also royally fucked.

Merthyr turned round, and Rudolph's fear was not alleviated by the comely smile she had affected. She looked crazier than a bucket of frogs, and that was seemingly her resting face. Her hair was peppered all about with bits of fungi and slush from the trough; a whole mushroom was skewered onto the end of one antler.

"Um, how is training going?" Rudolph just about managed between panicked swallows. She had put herself in the middle of the stable now, between Rudolph and the doors. At least, Rudolph *hoped* the doors were still there, for he could not see beyond the veritable beast of a cow now staring at him like he was dessert.

"It went," said she, "about as well as expected." The creepy smile remained, but her brow was furrowed now, and that combination was even more terrifying.

And then it was gone.

And Merthyr seemed to brighten, as if twenty kilos had suddenly dropped off her, or out of her. "Yeah, it wasn't bad," she said, almost sang—*"it wasn't baaaaaad, ooohhhh, it wasn't baaaad, ooooh, and so on."*—and Rudolph felt the temperature change in the stable. It had been chilly-cold a moment ago, and now it was pleasant. "I'll hopefully be transferred to Rink Two soon, so we'll be seeing a lot more of each other, my little Rudy!"

Rudolph laughed a little, although he hadn't meant to. It had fallen out of him involuntarily, and he wished, as he saw Merthyr's expression change once again, he could catch it and force it back into his stupid mouth, but he couldn't. It was too late.

"Something funny about that, little Rudy?" Merthyr asked, and was there a hint of Scottish lilt in that accent? Rudolph didn't know, because he'd never met a Scottish person before, but had he, and had he known what one sounded like, he might now be nodding and saying, Yes, *definitely* a highlander, and make no mistake.

"I... I was just thinking..." It was no use. Rudolph could produce no reasonable excuse for his rude laughter. It was perhaps best just to let her eat him now. Just lie down, hand her a knife and fork, and tell her to get on with it, but please leave his genitals for last.

"I'm just playing with you!" she said in what could only be described as an eruption. "Oh, baby Rudolph, you are so funny. And also so *weak*! And I wouldn't have it any other way!" And she did flickings of her perm; the mushroom from her antler flew across the stable and landed, fortuitously, back in the trough.

Rudolph's flabber was truly gasted, and he was also relieved. "I *am* funny!" he said, wishing she would just go away, silently praying that some terrible accident befell her during that afternoon's session. The thought that she might plunge to her death from two-hundred feet—the result of a mid-air coronary—should not have made him so excited, and yet it did, and also fearful for those poor souls at ground level who might suffer dearly from such an unfortunate event.

"So," she said, and Rudolph saw that she had stopped laughing once again. She had more moods than a hen-night, this one. "Tell me a joke, babeh Rudy," she said, and also, "and better make it a funny one, ya wee fanny."

It appeared that the more intense Merthyr became, so did the severity of her Scottishness.

Rudolph had the key to survival in his lap; the notebook, open and ready to pluck from in order to avoid a drubbing at the hooves of a potential lunatic, but no matter how hard he searched, he couldn't for the life of him find anything he thought that could be classified as a 'funny one, ya wee fanny'.

"Ach," said Merthyr, running out of patience quicker than Harold Shipman (way too soon, ed.?). "Ya couldnae make me laugh if yer held me down and tickled my pickle with your antlers."

"Cariboo!" Rudolph spat, for he had figured out the punchline to the last joke in his notes.

Merthyr, of course, didn't get it, and aptly wore the expression of someone who didn't get it. It was the same look Medusa's severed head gave to King Polydectes just before he turned to stone. Rudolph quickly checked about his person, just to make sure he was still made of flesh and fur and hadn't taken on the smooth aspect of a kitchen countertop.

He hadn't, thank fuck.

BABY RUDOLPH

"What do reindeers dress as for Halloween?" said Rudolph, the apple in his throat bobbing up and down like the blonde bird at the beginning of *Jaws*.

"Cariboo," said Merthyr, quite unimpressed. "Aye, you do know you have to put the punchline at the end, ya southern softie."

Rudolph nodded. "Of course," he said. "So, what do you think? Not a bad little rib-tickler that one, hm?"

Merthyr appeared to chew it over. "Oh, aye, aye," she said, grumpily, yet that grim smile was still there. A thin line in which you could swipe your credit card to pay for all sorts of negativity.

But then the smile stretched upwards, as if hoisted at the corners by hidden wires. Rudolph checked the rafters for hidden imps, tugging at fishing-wire, for this was The Land of Christmas, and anything was possible.

Merthyr laughed now, and it was way over-the-top, exaggerated a little too much for Rudolph's liking, but at least she wasn't sitting on him, which was nice, or eating him, which was even nicer.

Her laughter, such was its overemphasis, had brought into the stable a throng of curious reindeer, come to see what all the fuss was about. Rudolph suddenly felt more than a little embarrassed, but he was also relieved. Merthyr couldn't do anything strange to him while there were witnesses. He was safe, for now.

"Ha!" said Blitzen, nudging past three other reindeer to get to the front of the crowd. "Well, well, well, what do we have here?" He glanced at Rudolph, and then at Merthyr, who was looking nervously at the straw at her hooves. "What's this?" he asked again. "The beginning of a terrible orgy?" And he laughed, and so did Dancer, and Prancer, and Vixen, too. "Merthyr and Rudolph, sitting in a stable..." He paused there as if to think, and then brightened when he had it. "Merthyr a-sucking on Rudolph's cable!"

More laughter erupted; one reindeer, a bull named Joe, passed out from all the excitement.

Rudolph stood and began to gather about his personal belongings, huffing as he pushed them into his training bag. "We weren't doing anything," he said, his voice barely audible over the cheering and jeering of the gathered herd. *Now I know how Monica Lewinsky felt*, Rudolph thought.

"Didn't know you were into fatties," Dancer said, miming a fat person as she waddled from one side of the stable to the other. Rudoph watched and was extremely offended by what was going on.

BABY RUDOLPH

Merthyr was looking only at him with saucer eyes and a tremulous bottom lip. No longer the potential menace she had been just a moment ago, she was silently imploring him to help, to say something, to protect her, and by God Rudolph couldn't just stand by and watch as his cohorts made fun of Merthyr, no matter if she was a giant fatty from the planet Psycho.

"Shut up, you absolute garden privets!"

The stable fell suddenly silent. It was the kind of silence usually reserved for the dropping of pins; somewhere amongst the herd, a solitary, high-pitched fart had the audacity to wreck the effect, but apart from that, the silence was the clichéd deafening.

Merthyr, whose head had been so low to the ground that it almost touched a recently placed turd, seemed gladdened by Rudolph's intervention, and she lifted her head up. Up in the rafters, two breathless imps clinging to fishing wire exchanged exhausted glances before collapsing against nearby struts.

The no-longer-laughing herd slowly backed out of the stable, muttering things about how they were only joking and that they hadn't really believed Rudolph and Merthyr to be fucking, that it was just a silly joke, and that certain people needed to learn to take one, for fuck's sake.

"Ha!" Blitzen said, trying to keep the party going, but a quick glance round told him the fun was over and that the proverbial policemen had arrived at the house, checked everyone for ID, decided the party was unlawful, and dismissed all involved with a warning and the threat of further action if someone should decide to kick it all off again. "Yes, well, I shall be off, too," he said. "Got a lot of flying to do this afternoon. A lot, indeed."

Before either of them knew what was happening, Merthyr and Rudolph were alone once again.

"Ugh," said the bull named Joe, groggily coming to in the food trough.

Apart from *him*, Rudolph and Merthyr were alone.

"No one has ever done anything like that for me before," whispered the big 'un, fluttering her eyelashes and generally trying to make herself pretty, which she wasn't, and before it is mentioned by some angry reviewer in an effort to denigrate one, this narrator finds *all* reindeers pretty, but this one wasn't. Fuck ugly, she was, inside and out.

Rudolph didn't know what to say, so he didn't bother.

BABY RUDOLPH

"You saved me, baby Rudolph," Merthyr continued, clutching at her pink cardigan as if the fleas contained therein were fairly causing her all sorts of discomfort. "You made them stop, and—"

"You're welcome!" Rudolph said, and he bounced past her, for he recognised a suitable time to make an exit, and that was it. "See ya!" He flew the last dozen feet of the stable and didn't stop flying until he reached the safety of Rink Two, almost half-a-mile away. If he'd had lucky stars about his person, he would have counted them.

Back in the stable, Merthyr smiled.

She smiled and clutched at her pink cardigan and smiled again.

"Love," she said with a beatific smile.

"I love him, so I do. Mah babeh Rudy!"

A semi-conscious bull named Joe threw up into the lichen and fungi.

6

Machines rumbled and bleeped and whirred, a thousand of them, each doing something, some doing more than others, which is the way of any industrial unit, and also true of its workers, for there were those who toiled and sweated and barely stopped to take a breath, and then there were those lazy bastards, who spent much of the day next to the tea-urn or masturbating in the toilet cubicles over the current newspaper's page three.

Then there was Finklefoot, whose job it was to drag the lazy masturbating ones from the toilet cubicles by the pointy ear and set them back to work, whether they'd had time to put their little elf cock away or not.

The main hub of The Land of Christmas numbered two-thousand employees and—

"Ahhh!" screeched a voice as it went round and round a heavy-duty pillar drill.

The Land of Christmas's main manufactural hub, whose workforce numbered one-thousand-nine-hundred-and-ninety-nine, was, unlike the jigsaw factory, a hive of activity. Elves stood in front of machinery, loading in bits and bobs, taking out the same but in a far better configuration; conveyor belts ran for hundreds of metres, upon which, at regular intervals, were unpainted dolls, soon-to-be-painted dolls, half-painted dolls, and then fully painted dolls, for such was the way with conveyor belts, and once completed, off the dolls went to the boxing machines, where they would be encased first in formed plastic, and then stuffed into cardboard, before being stacked on pallets and ushered away by forklift trucks.

Amongst all of this busyness, Rat and Jimbo smoked their pipes and stuck the dots on dominoes, which was as important a job as any elf could hope to have.

Finklefoot, doing his rounds, stumbled upon them, and almost immediately wished he hadn't.

"Ooh, boss, boss!" said Rat, suddenly so distracted that he created an entirely new domino: the thirteen pipper.

"No," said Finklefoot, a-lighting his own pipe, for, having already dealt with seven frequent wanking wankers and one new to the hobby, he had earned it.

"You don't even know what I was gonna say, boss," Rat said.

"Yes, I do," replied Finklefoot, blowing smoke-rings that danced and pranced and fairly fluttered all about the place. "You were going to try to talk me into being a Bee Gee."

"He's good, intee?" said Jimbo. "I don't know how he does it."

"Think about it, boss," Rat said, pouring a fresh tea from a nearby urn. "*Stayin' Alive, Night Fever, You Should be Dancing.*"

"You should be *working*," said Finklefoot, of which he was relatively proud. "You're not going to change my mind, Rat, so you might as well quit while you're behind."

"I'll bet Trixie won't let him do it," Jimbo said. "That's what it is. He doesn't want to piss off the little lady at home, knowing how popular we'd be." He sucked thoughtfully upon his pipe before continuing. "Yes, the B*ee Gees* were known for making wet knickers, and our boss here doesn't want to ruffle the feathers of his jealous wife."

"I shall hit you with something in a minute," Finklefoot said, looking round for something to follow through with. "Trixie is not jealous in the slightest, and it is my decision not to take part in The Land of Christmas Annual Variety Show as the third wheel in a *Bee Gees* tribute band. And also, don't say anything negative about my wife. She is more than a woman—"

"See!" Rat gasped. "You're *perfect*. More than a woman, indeed."

Finklefoot silently berated himself. He should have seen that one coming a mile off.

As should we all.

"Look, boss," Jimbo said as he nudged a bucket of completed dominoes across the factory floor with his foot. "We need to get this thing going soon. The show is next week, and we haven't even started rehearsing yet, since there's no point with just the two of us."

"There were two for a while," Finklefoot said, not quite knowing where he was going with this. "After Maurice died—"

"Oh, yeah!" Rat said. You wouldn't think you could squeeze so much sarcasm into just two words, but there you have it. "We can be the Bee Gees *after* Maurice died! That'll have the women squirting in the aisles."

"Doesn't sound great, does it?" added Jimbo, for it didn't.

"No, we need three of us to make a decent *Bee Gees*," Rat went on. And on and on and on, Finklefoot thought, for he was growing rather tired of all this nonsense.

Just then, the tannoy made a silly noise—like a beep and a honk had a baby, and the subsequent bonk was not all there, mentally speaking—and a voice they all knew well cleared its throat and said:

"Sorry to interrupt your toiling, gentlemen, but I need the assistance of your foreman in a rather delicate matter." And then, after a few seconds had passed, in which no one had moved a muscle, the voice boomed: "Get your fucking backside to my office, Finklefoot. Now!"

The tannoy squawked, as tannoys are wont to do, and then the factory was filled with conspiratorial mutterings—*mumble, mumble, mumble, rhubarb, rhubarb, mumble*—from the bit players.

"That was The Fat Bastard," Jimbo said. "Shit, Finklefoot, what have you done?"

Finklefoot thought carefully. And as he thought, and involuntarily shook, Rat and Jimbo watched him the way one might watch a bomb that had just ticked over into its final minute.

"I haven't done anything!" said Finklefoot, tamping and pocketing his pipe. "At least, not that I'm aware of."

Jimbo shrugged. "Then you have nothing to worry about," he said.

BABY RUDOLPH

Ten minutes and a thousand tiny steps later, Finklefoot stood in front of The Fat Bastard. The office, for reasons unbeknownst to Finklefoot, carried the scent of Grimsby.

"Nothing to worry about," said Santa from behind his heaving desk, for it was so heavily laden with paper that it buckled in the middle. "I just need your assistance with something."

Finklefoot sighed. If relief were visible, it would have been seen to jump from the foreman's mouth, rush across the room, and perform a little dance before leaving through the half-open office door.

"Assist you with something?" Finklefoot asked. "Yes, quite, of course."

Santa, aka Jovial TheeJerkoff, poured himself a large Scotch and offered Finklefoot the same.

"Not while I'm foremanning," said the important elf, for he knew a potential trap when he saw one.

"It has come to my attention," Santa said, "that Ahora is missing. As of this morning, her whereabouts remains unknown, and the jigsaw factory is, how should I put it, about as empty as a hermit's address book." He leaned back in his chair and it creaked as if to say, *Haven't you heard of salads, for crying out loud?*

Finklefoot frowned. It wasn't like Ahora to throw a sickie without giving a month's notice first, and it certainly wasn't like her to allow work at the jigsaw factory to grind to a halt. She was just as strict as Finklefoot when it came to her workers; the only difference being that her wankers were mainly female, and utilisation of the factory cubicles for such activities during the day was not only tolerated but recommended. According to Ahora, it helped with productivity. Jigsaw pieces, fiddly as they were, were far easier to handle with semi-sticky fingers. Which was why new jigsaw puzzles came with that special smell.

"And she's not at home?" Finklefoot said, not that it was any of his business. In fact, he couldn't think of one reason this had anything to do with him at all.

The Fat Bastard shook his head. "I sent a couple of elves out to check," he said, sipping furtively from his glass. "They knocked and knocked, but she didn't answer."

Hm.

Finklefoot, armed with this added information, said, "I hope you don't mind me asking, sir, but..." Like a slug on an out-of-control children's roundabout, he trailed off there.

"Why you?" Santa asked, getting the gist of what Finklefoot was aiming for.

BABY RUDOLPH

"Why me, sir?"

"Yes, well," said The Fat Bastard, "I was sitting here this morning, running it all through my head, and coming up empty."

"Like the OceanGate submarine," said Finklefoot.

"Indeed," said Santa without even a chortle. "Anyway, the more I thought about it, the more it reminded me of... dare I say it, the more it brought back memories of that awful incident a decade ago."

Finklefoot shuddered, for he had been trying for the past ten years to *forget* the whole thing with Krampus and the other companions, and that terrible Santapede thingamajig, with all the elves having to eat shit, and then shit into the mouths of those in the chain behind them, and... well, you can see why he was trying to forget all about it. It was hardly a happy little wet dream, unless that sort of thing floats your boat. However, if you should want to find out more about the terrible incident, *The Human Santapede* is available in all formats from the usual suspects and makes a wonderfully festive Christmas present for those children you can't stand.

"You remember it?" Santa went on. "That nasty business with Krampus?"

"All too well," said Finklefoot, dry-swallowing, for every drop of fluid had left his mouth, and it didn't half hurt just to gulp.

"Yes, well, I remembered the part you played in bringing that whole debacle to a satisfying conclusion, and I thought, You know who I need on this case? There's only one elf brave enough and tough enough for the job."

While Finklefoot did enjoy the sensation of smoke being blown up his arse, he wasn't a major fan of hyperbole or manipulation tactics. It was a swings-and-roundabouts thing, and Finklefoot knew when a large knife had been pulled out and smothered with Flora with the intention of buttering him up.

"I'd rather not get involved," said Finklefoot. "I might have been a little lucky to survive that Santapede caper, and wouldn't want to give the bastards, *any* bastards, in fact, a second opportunity to finish me off."

"I thought you'd say that," said The Fat Bastard, pushing himself up from the long-suffering chair. "Which is why I've decided to outlaw reluctant elves entirely. Any unwillingness to take part in *anything* shall be discerned as treason, and therefore punishable by exile to Earth. Your free will,

BABY RUDOLPH

Finklefoot, has been rescinded, and will only be returned to you once this mission is satisfactorily concluded."

"I thought you'd say that," said Finklefoot, for he had. "So does that mean I'm to search for Ahora post-haste, sir, only I've a factoryfull of elves that usually benefit from my presence, as foreman, and whatnot."

"My wife has agreed to look after them until you return," said The Fat Bastard.

I'll bet she did, Finklefoot thought, for he was fully aware of her small-person fetish and her proclivity to collect as many of them as possible in her little black book, as if they were the sexual equivalent of Pokemon. So far, he had managed to avoid her advances, but it was only a matter of time...

"In fact," Santa continued, "she was rather *fond* of the idea, so I suggest you hurry up and get this case sorted before Jessica gets a grip of things down there."

Already has by now, Finklefoot thought as his gaze fell upon the wall clock to Santa's rear. Her grip would have gotten dozens of his workers by now. The thought of a queue, snaking all the way back through the factory but culminating at the toilets, made Finklefoot shake his head.

Slut, he thought.

"I'll get right on it, sir," Finklefoot said, and was halfway to the office door when something occurred to him, and he turned back.

"Sir, why not go to the police with this?" he asked. "I mean, they were installed, were they not, following the events of last decade, to deal with things of this nature, should they ever arise."

The Fat Bastard shrugged. "Yes, well, I've spoken with Captain Quim of the LCPD this very morning, and he mentioned something about a missing persons report and a forty-eight hour cooling-off-period, or suchlike, and how they usually turn up dead, so why bother looking for them in the first place if that's all they're going to do. Wouldn't it be much better to wait for them to turn up, and then you can claim that you found them, albeit a little late, and get all the credit? It's a remarkable way of thinking, and I told Quim as much, before I promoted him to Chief."

"Makes sense," said Finklefoot, turning for the door once again.

I'm surrounded by fucking idiots, he thought as he left Santa's office.

7

Down in the basement, Ahora sobbed, for there wasn't much else to do. Her captor had left her nothing with which to entertain herself, and there was only so many times you could beat yourself at I-Spy, especially when most of the things she would have been able to spy were covered in darkness. We'll leave her there, because it's quite boring just to watch a captive elf cry for any period of time. Just remember she's there; it's important for later. Maybe.

*

Policing in The Land of Christmas was a relatively new idea, but as with anything, things must start somewhere, and this particular thing was born from Krampus's deviancy a decade previous. Shouldn't there, the consensus was, be somewhere to go to report crimes, as exceedingly rare as they might be, and therefore create a safer Land to live in for all and sundry?

It was a fine idea, and one which had passed across the desk of The Fat Bastard with very little fanfare, but within a fortnight of signing off on it, a station had popped up in the High Street, and two elves had enthusiastically voluonteered to man the station and deal with all the criminality that came their way, usually by way of a token fine, welcome bribery, and a slap on the wrist.

Bob Dufflecoat, now Officer Dufflecoat, was quite tall for an elf. He had about him a touch of the Sherlocks, which was to say his nose was hooked and he wore a deerstalker and smoked a gourd Calabash, even though it was terribly bad for his health and made him cough like a stage-four cancer victim. He had affected this image almost immediately after taking up the role, and it was far too late now to get rid of it without looking like a complete tool.

Chief Quim, newly promoted, wore a tan suit with patches in the elbows and a matching tie, of which he had seven sets, one for each day of the week, a rule which he seldom enforced. Unlike his colleague and subordinate, Chief Quim had opted for the CSI look, for nothing struck fear into the hearts and minds of criminals quite like a man dressed up like a Geography teacher.

BABY RUDOLPH

These men, these proponents of law and order—and also of sitting around and not doing much of anything, really, for the pay was already reasonable, so why spoil a good thing?—were sitting behind their respective desks when an elf entered and said:

"Any news on the case of the missing Ahora?"

Officer Dufflecoat looked at Chief Quim.

Chief Quim looked at Officer Dufflecoat.

Finklefoot looked at them both and thought, *Tossers*.

"The missing elf," said Chief Quim, not a question. "We have done all we can concerning that case," he said, and he took up a giant mug of coffee from his desk and slurped from it.

"So," Finklefoot said, glancing about the place and admiring the general... absence of things. Apart from a solitary picture hanging on the wall—a recent of Ahora, holding up a jigsaw piece and looking rather proud of herself—there wasn't much at all to look at. "You're just going to sit there for the next forty-eight hours? Until a missing-persons report can be filed?"

Officer Dufflecoat nodded and filled his Calabash. "It would appear that our hands, as it were, are tied. Of course, there's the possibility that she'll save us the bother by turning up dead, but that's out of our hands."

Finklefoot was taken so far aback, he knocked over a dormant photocopier. "You can't be serious," he said. "There is an elfnapper out there, a murderer, maybe, and one of our Land's finest has been taken. Tooketh, she is, and this is how our beloved LCPD acts?"

"What's it to you, anyway?" Chief Quim asked, fiddling with his tie. "You a nosey bastard?"

"Think of me as an elf on a mission," said Finklefoot, which he quite liked the sound of. "I'm taking over this case with immediate effect, and I would very much like it if you two—" Don't say it, don't say it, don't say it, "—gentlemen would assist me until such a time arrives that you have anything better to do."

Arseholes.

"As we've already made clear," Chief Quim said, producing a plastic lunchbox from his top drawer and helping himself to its contents; what appeared to be turkey sandwiches, "there's not much more we can do until the forty-eight hours are up, and then we're obligated to check the usual places. The dark alleyways and park toilets, that sort of thing, anywhere a body might show up dead and—"

BABY RUDOLPH

"Well, aren't you about as useful as a pipe-cleaner on the Mersey tunnel," Finklefoot said. His stomach rumbled as he watched the Chief nosh into his turkey sandwiches. "There must be something you can do. Or at least some way you can assist me, so that *I* can do something."

Officer Dufflecoat suddenly became animated, which was not a bad idea for a Christmas special. "Krampus!" he said. "That's who you need to be talking to. He knows a thing or two about making people disappear."

Now, the atmosphere in the room had altered; it was as if all the oxygen had been sucked out with one of those cordless, bagless whatchamacallits and replaced with something far less breathable. Giraffe farts, perhaps. Chief Quim was miming that 'cut-it-off' gesture to Dufflecoat, but when Finklefoot turned to catch him in the act, he returned to his turkey sandwich, pretending he hadn't been doing anything in the first place.

"Krampus?" frowned Finklefoot. His tongue itched now, as if the mere mention of Santa's evil counterpart had left nits on its surface.

"Um, no, forget I said anything," Officer Dufflecoat backtracked. "I've been smoking a new tobacco, and I'm not quite sure it's one-hundred-percent legal, if you know what I mean. Lots of little green bits in it, and it's made my lips looser than an elf of the night's flange."

Finklefoot shook his head so hard that he made himself a tad dizzy. "No, you know something I don't," he said. "Something about Krampus."

"All I know is that he's a bloody big bugger and he likes to do bad things to good elves," Dufflecoat said. "I was only an elfling when he did what he did, but I have read the book, still available, I believe, from all good booksellers, and everything I know about that malevolent companion, I got it from there." He made a Scout's Honour sign, and then the sign of the cross.

Like regular sex, Finklefoot was having none it. "You *know* something, and I want to know what it is, otherwise I shall have to take up matters with everyone's least favourite potentate."

As if he'd been threatened with defenestration from a fiftieth-floor window, Officer Dufflecoat said, "He's underneath us!"

"Oh, for fuck's sake!" Chief Quim said, slamming both fists down on his desk. The turkey slice hanging from the corner of his mouth took away from his wrath. How could

BABY RUDOLPH

anyone be fearful of an elf wearing twenty grammes of Bernard Matthews' finest sandwich filler.

"What do you mean, he's underneath us?" Finklefoot asked. "Krampus was banished to Earth to live out the remainder of his existence in human form and as the leader of the Conservative Party."

"He wasn't," said Officer Dufflecoat.

Chief Quim slammed his hands down yet again. This time he accidentally caught the lip of his lunch-box. "Does 'sworn to secrecy' mean anything to you, Officer?" he said, picking a cherry tomato out of his eye socket.

Officer Dufflecoat shrugged and lit his pipe. Plumes of blue smoke rose into the air; a thin wisp of it, in the shape of a question mark, hovered momentarily over Finklefoot before fizzling out. "Well," he said, "this little fella needs help, and if anyone knows about elfnappers, it's Krampus."

Last year, Finklefoot's wife, Trixie, had frightened the absolute life out of him when, upon his return from a particularly tough day at work—three deaths, seven major accidents, and somehow a dog had got into the factory and made a nuisance of itself, as they invariably do—she had informed him of an odd feeling within her. Having been lucky enough to get away with it for over a century, there was a good chance, she informed him, that he was, that they *both* were, about to experience something of an upheaval. I believe, she had told him, that the impromptu encounter they'd both played their parts in three Sundays prior (helluva nice way to describe a quickie while their dinner was in the microwave) might have left her with a bun in the oven. The relief Finklefoot felt that night when it turned out to be just a massive shit, oh! *Wonderful*, it had been.

The feeling he currently had was exactly like the moment his wife sprung the possibility of an elfling on him; horrible, it was.

"You're telling me you have Krampus beneath this building, right now, as we speak?"

Officer Dufflecoat nodded; his deerstalker tried to do a runner off the side of his head. "Precisely," he said, straightening his hat and trying desperately not to make eye contact with his superior, whose scowl was enough to frighten crows away.

Finklefoot couldn't believe it. Why hadn't The Fat Bastard mentioned this to him? Why keep Krampus and his incarceration a secret for all these years? Like a bag of potatoes that had pushed out so many little sprouts, he had been kept in the dark, and he wasn't best pleased about it.

BABY RUDOLPH

"He is in a *cage*, I take it," Finklefoot said.

"Actually, he's in a bulletproof glass cell," said Chief Quim. "One of those with the little holes in it. He does like a natter, does Krampus. Dufflecoat here sometimes reads him a bedtime story—"

"I'm going to have to speak with him," Finklefoot said.

Right after I've changed my underpants, he thought.

*

That afternoon, Rudolph couldn't fly for toffee. The session had started badly with three runway overshoots and one near-miss with a flock of pigeons. From there, it had all been downhill. A new exercise, flying headlong into a series of 5G radio waves, had resulted in a bout of mid-air unconsciousness, and Rudolph had been lucky to wake up in the seconds before impact, and safely perform an emergency landing in which he lost a bit off one of his antlers.

He couldn't shake the feeling that he was being watched.

And not by the other reindeer on Rink Two, no, this was someone else, somewhere else, and it was playing silly buggers with his concentration. If you've ever passed through customs, completely innocent and yet, for some reason, full to the brim with paranoia, and all of a sudden you've forgotten how to walk in a straight line, and fuck, what if someone's put something illicit in your suitcase while you weren't looking, and now the customs officers are regarding you the same way a hungry lion does a well-toned gladiator, then you'll know precisely the feeling Rudolph was experiencing.

Up there amongst the snow-filled clouds, it was difficult to see much at ground level, especially when he was moving about the place at almost half the speed of light, but occasionally, he could have sworn he caught the slightest glimpse of a pink cardigan, the brief flash of a chubby perm, and the grim slit of a psychotic smile somewhere down there, through the heavy snow.

It's your imagination, he had told himself, but it was like trying to convince a leper not to get scabs all over the place. They're going to do it, anyway.

When the whistle went to call an end to proceedings, Rudolph was glad of it. He wanted to get out of there as quickly as possible, so forfeited the after-training shower, thanked the coach for not tearing him a new one for his piss-poor performance, grabbed his bag and left.

BABY RUDOLPH

When he arrived back at his personal stable—a twelve-by-twelve enclosure just outside the town centre—he was a nervous wreck, and convinced that someone had been following him.

"Pull yourself together," he whispered as he took out a carrot from the fridge and took it across to his desk, plonked himself down, booted up his laptop, the usual.

Now, once again, suspend disbelief. If a reindeer can write in scruffy cursive using a fifty-pence biro, they can certainly type on a qwerty keyboard without smooshing all the keys at once and accidentally producing a new E.L. James novel.

The Wi-Fi wasn't great in The Land of Christmas (and would never be great, since they were literally hijacking it from Earth, in the adjacent dimension, and they were grateful at least for the fact that one of them, may years ago, had guessed the password correctly) but it didn't take long for Rudolph, putting up with the machine screeching and beeping for a minute or so, to connect to the Elfernet.

He took a big bite of his carrot and logged into MyFace.

He had a couple of hours to spare before a secret—hopefully not so secret that no one turned up—underground gig in which he planned to test out his new material, do the bit about coconut Putin, maybe finish with the Halloween joke, the world, as they say, was his oyster. He was nervous, but also looking for—

"What the fuck?" he said, and then, in case anyone missed it the first time, he added, "What the fuck?"

Rudolph was popular on the app. Of course he was, he was one of The Fat Bastard's favourite substitutes, the deer of the hour, the guy that gets shit done when the fog gets too treacherous. As one of the most famous inhabitants of The Land of Christmas, it was no surprise that people wanted to connect with him. There were, of course, hundreds of bot accounts, and Rudolph could spot these a mile off. You didn't need an illuminating red nose to see that Barbie, 27, whose profile picture consisted of eighty percent tittage, twenty-percent duck-lips, was not in fact genuine. Rudolph received something in the way of a dozen friend requests from fake accounts daily, and he deleted these before they had the chance to make themselves comfortable, which left only genuine requests, which he liked to work through at his leisure, see if they were a good fit for him or if they were just going to ask him for money as soon as he hit confirm, the way they sometimes did.

BABY RUDOLPH

"No fucking way," said Rudolph, staring at the latest batch of requests, and one in particular, because it was none other than Merthyr Titful, that veritable scarer of all things smaller than her. Her profile picture was so filtered you could have added two sugars and some cream, made yourself a nice cappuccino. Her face took up the entire square, and she had her nose all scrunched up, trying to perhaps be cute but looking more like something had flown up into one of her nostrils and laid eggs.

Rudolph was about to delete the request when he realised something and stopped just in time.

Off in the distance a wolf howled. Whether that had anything to do with Rudolph's sudden change of heart, we'll never know, except it definitely was, and the wolf, translated, had just said, *Rather you than me.*

To delete Merthyr's request was like drawing a dick on her face while she was asleep and then waking her up to point it out. He would *have* to see her again, he just knew it, and what would he tell her when she mentioned the snub? *Oh, sorry, I don't go on there that much*, or, *Yeah, I only add people who don't look like they want to fuck me and then kill me, or flip it, kill first and then fuck.* He wouldn't be able to look her in the eyes again, which suited him fine, but he was quite sure she'd have a differing opinion.

"Fuck!" Rudolph said, his front hooves behind his head, and he just stared at the request, willing it away. Perhaps, if he concentrated hard enough, it would turn into a popup urging him to click For *Horny Barasinghas in Your Area Tonight!* but it didn't happen, no matter how hard he manifested.

There was only one way to make the friend request go away, and that was to accept it.

And so, with a febrile hoof and a twitching bumhole, he moved the mouse over the request and clicked it.

There was a moment—it could have been a minute, could have been an hour—between left-clicking the mouse and the page changing, in which several thoughts ran through Rudolph's mind. The first was: *maybe she's perfectly normal and I just caught her having a mental day.* We all have them, after all, and maybe Merthyr was currently in the throes of one. The second thought was: perhaps she would leave him alone now, now that he had accepted and she had access to him and his life on a digital level. Quite often, this was the case. Fans were desperate to add him to their menagerie, so that they might brag to their friends and families about it, but the novelty soon wore off when they realised he was no different to them. He lived an otherwise regular, unremarkable life, but made a cracking spaghetti bolognese. The third thought he had was: *how long is this page going to take to load?*

As if responding, the page loaded, and that was when the true nightmare began.

"Holy shit and what the fuck!"

Rudolph could hardly move; galvanised with fear, he was.

There was too much going on all at once, so he decided to take things one step at a time, beginning with the picture pinned at the top of her page.

It was a photograph of Rudolph, mid-air and upside-down, and had been taken that very same day at a distance. The caption accompanying the photograph was:

Here he is! My bewtiful babeh Rudolf. Doesn't he look cute? I deffo wud sit on that nose! Alreddy have.

"You fucking well have not!" said Rudolph, trying to hold down the gallon of sick currently holding counsel in his throat. He was shaking more, now, as uncontrollable rage and unmitigated fear decided to have an arm-wrestle. "What in Santa's empty sack is going on with this shit?"

The second photo was also of Rudolph. This time he was taking a break at the edge of the rink, drinking thirstily from a bottle and spilling it down his chin. It was one of those candid-type photos, like when they catch Ben Affleck wondering how the hell he'd gone so wrong in life and thinking to himself, *Perhaps I should go with a different name next time, and not just another Jennifer.* The caption to this post was:

Aye! Look at him. Can't wait to be drippin' doon his chin later. Make nae mistake aboot it.

Like he'd just woken from some terrible nightmare, Rudolph was all at once paler than an albino poltergeist and shaking like a shitting chihuahua. "This can't be happening," he whisper grunted. And what made it worse was that her posts had hundreds of likes, loves, comments and reposts. Rudolph scrolled down the thread and was amazed by what people were saying: *Aw, you make a lovely couple.* And, *Oh, you deserve a nice lad, Merthyr.* And, *Lucky girl. I'd give my left labia lip for one night with Rudolph.*

BABY RUDOLPH

That last one was from Jessica Claus.

"This isn't happening!" Rudolph gasped. "No, no, no, this can't be real!"

But it was... *very* real, and as if to prove how very real it was, there were a dozen further posts of the same ilk, all showing Rudolph in various flying positions, or sitting positions. There was even one of him covertly shitting at the back of the water vending machine. Each photo was accompanied by a post from Merthyr. *Look at how graceful my wee man is!* And, *If you think he looks athletic in these, you shud see him in the bedroom.* And, *Look at ma sexy wee man taking a wee shite*!

As if it would somehow make everything go away, Rudolph logged out quickly and sat staring at MyFace login page for an interminable amount of time. He only realised he'd stopped blinking when a drunken fly collided with his retina, and even then he had to consciously make an effort to blink it away like the least willing windscreen wipers on the market.

It'll be okay, he told himself. Merthyr was just a little strange, that's all, and had taken something of a shine to him, which was to be expected from someone of her... standard? To someone like Merthyr, even a two was a seven, and therefore out of her league, and so a ten like Rudolph, obviously, would appear almost Godlike to her. *But God and goblin do not go together*, Rudolph thought, at least not in the real world they don't. Despite what Merthyr's profile said, Rudolph would make it clear he was not currently having, nor ever had, sexual relations with that reindeer.

"Crazy bitch," said Rudolph.

He started to get himself ready for the secret stand-up show, where he could forget all about Merthyr Titful and do what he did second-best.

Make people sort of laugh.

BABY RUDOLPH

8

Finklefoot stood at one end of a long corridor, scratching at his beard and trying to figure out how something so big and long could be built beneath the LCPD's only and much smaller one-roomed station. It was ridiculous, and went against all rules of space, and perhaps even time, as it would take a bloody fair bit of it just to walk down to the other end. You could hold a decathlon down here, Finklefoot thought, and still have space left over for a fishing pond.

"Why's it so cold down here?" asked Finklefoot. His voice echoed round the corridor and came back to him well-travelled.

"Over-ceiling cooling," said Chief Quim. "From all the snow up there, you know?"

Finklefoot did know; he'd seen enough of it to last him a lifetime, and it had. "So where is he?" he asked, suddenly wishing he were somewhere—*anywhere!*—else.

"He's down at the other end," said Officer Dufflecoat. "All the way down there." He pointed with a tremulous finger into the distance.

"Bit silly, that," said Finklefoot, looking at the empty cell just to their left. You could have stuck him in there and saved your little legs." *And saved mine at the same time*, he thought but didn't say.

"It's best he's as far away as possible," Chief Quim said, wiping mustard from his grey beard with his tie. "On account that he freaks us both out."

"Right," Finklefoot said, rather cheerfully, considering the circumstances. "I'll be off, then," and he started along the corridor on legs that felt like wet noodles.

"Stay to the right," Dufflecoat whispered after him.

"Why?" asked Finklefoot, stopping suddenly. "I thought you said he was behind unbreakable glass."

"He is," said Chief Quim. "We've just had the corridor floor re-concreted on the left and we don't want prints of your size twos as a permanent fixture."

Yes, quite, Finklefoot thought, for it was an awful gag.

He moved slowly along the corridor, passing empty cell after empty cell and thinking what a waste of taxpayer money it really was. Also, there were enough empty cells down here to eradicate homelessness thrice over. He made a mental note to mention that to The Fat Bastard when he got the chance, and then scratched it almost as quickly when he realised that not many elves, homeless or otherwise, would fancy bedding down every night next to someone as evil as Krampus. *Probably couldn't pay them to sleep down here*, Finklefoot thought. Ungrateful bastards, the homeless.

As he walked, and walked, and walked, it occurred to him how useful it would be to have one of those speedy, wheeled things they apparently handed out like candy to little people on Earth. What was it that made dwarves so bastard lazy, anyway? They moved quicker than buggery when there was a pantomime audition or if George Lucas was in town, but catch them on their downtime and all of a sudden they can't walk for toffee. Just Finklefoot's opinion, of course, and not that of, say, an otherworldly biographer.

"Almost there!" came the sudden announcement from Officer Dufflecoat, which made Finklefoot jump and almost topple over to the left, where his terrified features would have been captured for eternity like an inverse Han Solo in Carbonite. (Last *Star Wars* reference now, lest litigation ensue. ed.)

Finklefoot approached the corridor's end with trepidation, and also heavy shorts, for he was about to be reacquainted with the creature of his nightmares (also, last alternative *Blink 182* lyric. ed.) and he was fairly shaken up about the whole thing.

The last few feet seemed to take an hour to cover, but then Krampus came slowly into view, one horn, ten fangs, three claws at a time. Finklefoot fought the urge to turn round and make a run for it; the reenforced glass didn't look anything special from where he was standing, and the beast on the other side of it looked like he could quite easily smash through it, should he so desire, and desire he no doubt did.

Now standing fully before the monster, Finklefoot dry-swallowed and said, "All right, mate?"

Huge, he was, and all sharp edges and fur. He could give a Swiss army knife a run for its money, could Krampus, and Finklefoot couldn't quite believe that a decade ago, he had gone toe-to-toe with the gigantic bastard in what has now been consigned to the history books as *The Human Santapede*. What a silly bugger he'd been, back then. And also, what a silly bugger he was right now, putting himself in front of his mortal enemy once again, and saying something stupid like, *All right, mate.*

Krampus didn't move a muscle, which was a good thing, because if he had whole empires might have fallen,

BABY RUDOLPH

earthquakes might have torn through the land, and Jessica Claus might have fallen off her pole.

"Erm," Finklefoot said, trying not to make eye-contact. "Erm, yes, well, I was wondering, well—"

"You're the little bastard that put me here," growled Krampus with one of those voices made up of hundreds, nay *thousands*, of daemon voices. It wasn't quite deep enough to cause terrible earthquakes, but up on the surface, an elegant tea-party lost a saucer and a cube of sugar leapt from its bowl.

"Well, yes, of *course* you would remember me," Finklefoot said, looking for the Emergency Exit. "But let us put that aside for now, shall we?"

"Ten years of incarceration," said Krampus, "and he wants to put it aside. Ten years I've been in this shitforsaken glass box, like a recalcitrant tarantula, and he wants to just 'put it aside'." He was moving now, and the earth it did shaketh, and the creatures they did runneth, and things of that biblical nature. "A decade of my life gone, and don't even get me started on the food down here. I've had better meals on a Jet2 holiday." He threw a plastic tray across the cell, and it clattered against the far wall, an action that would have been somewhat scary had the tray been made from porcelain and the wall been made of more porcelain. As it was, once the tray came to rest, there was really nothing at all frightening about it at all.

"I'm sorry about what happened back then" lied Finklefoot. "It was a long time ago, and you were up to no good, what with stitching all those beings together, arse-to-face."

Krampus turned on his heels, of which there were countless. It was hard to make out all the limbs and claws and fangs in a biological sense and as a whole. Best to just look at the whole mass and admit that, yes, it *was* rather fucking nasty.

"What do you want from me, elf?" roared the beast. Up on the surface, an elderly elf fell from her chair and spilled an entire Lipton's green tea into her face.

"A woman has gone missing. A female elf, rather, I don't know what we're calling them these days." Finklefoot didn't, but a certain otherworldly biographer should by now. He was none-the-wiser, also.

"An elfnapper?" Krampus licked his goat lips and fingered one of his horns. "Oh! *Music* to my ears!"

Finklefoot shrugged. Had he thought this would go any other way? Of course not. Everything was as he'd imagined, and bang on schedule.

BABY RUDOLPH

"And you want me to point you in the direction of the villain," continued the half-man, half-goat, all-bastard, "and therefore the location of this missing elf, am I hearing that right?"

Once again, Finklefoot shrugged. "It'd be ever so helpful," he said. "Not to mention the fact it would make me go away."

Krampus laughed at this. Up on the surface, a paisley curtain unfastened itself from its window restraints and dropped to the floor as if it had been assassinated. And then he roared:

"Quid pro quo, Finklefoot! Quid pro quo!"

For a moment, Finklefoot said nothing. What could he say? He didn't even speak German.

"It means," said Krampus, sensing he had lost the little bastard, "you scratch my balls, and I'll not scratch your eyes out."

"Ah!" Finklefoot said, as if he understood, when in fact it was quite the opposite.

Krampus clicked his tongue and did shakings of his magnificent goat head. "I'll do something for you, but I expect a fucking favour in return," he said, as clearly and without hidden connotations as possible.

"Yes, right!" said Finklefoot. "Quite, of course. Well, I'm not in any position to negotiate with you, but I could certainly ask someone, as it were, to throw you a bone."

That appeared to be enough for Krampus, and he became a different monster altogether. "Then I would like a view," he said, "of the Sydney Opera House, and also the Taj Mahal. I would like to watch England win in the final of a major tournament, and witness the moment a distant star goes supernova. I want to be able to listen to the music of Mozart, live at the point of creation. I want a golden dragon egg, and also two-ply toilet paper, because my claws go through the stuff they've been giving me, and it takes forever to clean my nails."

"You're taking the piss," said Finklefoot, for he knew a silly bugger when he saw one; usually it involved a mirror.

"Not about the toilet paper," he said, holding up shit-encrusted talons. "Do that for me, and I'll give you your elfnapper and save the girl."

"I think I can manage that," Finklefoot said, and off he went in search of two-ply bog roll. When he returned, he placed it into the tray and pushed it through to the other side.

Krampus removed the toilet paper and hugged it as if it were a long-lost child. He then dragged himself across the cell toward a small, aluminium toilet jobby, and was about to sit down when Finklefoot said, "Can that wait until I've left? It's hard enough looking at you as it is, without watching you crimp one off."

"Your missing elf," he said, completely ignoring Finklefoot's whining and sitting right on down, "is somewhere she shouldn't be. A place of ill intent, somewhere unfamiliar to her. Have the lambs stopped screaming yet?"

"What?"

"Sorry. Don't know what came over me," said Krampus just as something heavy and solid made a thump noise somewhere beneath him.

Finklefoot looked pleadingly at the myriad tiny holes in the unbreakable glass, willing them to shrivel up before the inevitable smell escaped through them.

"She is frightened, Finklefoot, so scared she could *gnnnn*!" His dark cheeks were now red, and a small river of sweat ran down his nose and dripped onto the cell floor.

"Oh, come on!" Finklefoot said. "Shit later, for crying out loud. Tell me something about the bodysnatcher so I can be off and leave you to poop in peace."

Krampus wiped and flushed, commended Finklefoot on his appropriate choice of good bog-roll and hefted himself back onto all-fours.

"Your elfnapper," he said, "is something of an enigma, a puzzle within a riddle sitting on top of a question mark."

Finklefoot wanted to smite the sonofabitch; no wonder he'd won that battle all those years ago. Pure rage had no doubt played a part, for Krampus was insufferable.

"I'm seeing someone—" he placed a cloven-but-clawed whateveryoucallit against his head and closed his eyes; the mime of the piss-taking psychic, "—who likes to take things that don't belong to them—"

"Okay!" Finklefoot said, turning on his heels and marching away. "We're done! We're done here!"

Krampus called him back with an actual roar. Up on the surface, snow refused to land for a few seconds, and a seasoned masturbator in the toilet cubicle of Finklefoot's factory ripped his little elf-cock right off.

Finklefoot rushed back to the glass cell, expecting a sudden onslaught of valuable information, an incredible change of heart from the monstrous former companion as he spewed out impossible-to-know particulars that would, invariably, lead to the capture of the elfnapper and the safe return of Ahora of the Jigsaw Factory.

So, when Krampus said, "Can you ask them for a plunger? I appear to have filled this lavatory," Finklefoot was more disappointed than the man who bought the DVD about disappointment, only to open it to find the disc missing.

The torturous corridor walk back, accompanied by Krampus's Hellish laughter, was enough to drive an elf insane. By the time he got back to ground level, said his goodbyes to Quim and Dufflecoat, and made his way out into the snow, he really was quite mad.

Cut to...

*

INT. A DARK BASEMENT - NIGHT (or thereabouts)

The room is no bigger than the last time we checked in, and also no smaller, which was how rooms invariably worked unless something had been done to them, either through magic or sledgehammer. A barred cell upon which you could play Jingle Bells if you hit the right bars in the right sequence, and in that cell a broken woman-elf. She is tired, hungry, thirsty, and very annoyed with her captor.

Speaking of which, there they sit at a sewing machine. In the background, *Goodbye Horses* by Q Lazzarus plays on an old, dusty Gramophone. The figure is hunched over the sewing machine as if broken-backed. They are concentrating as they feed material carefully through the Singer (no relation to Bryan).

Ahora, our captive, watches through the cell bars. She is also humming along to the music now, for it ain't half a catchy tune. She can see her captor working away at the sewing machine, makes a mental note of the pink cardigan they are wearing, as if it matters in some way, but that is all her abductor is wearing. From the waist down they are stark-bollock naked.

Stark clam naked?

Utter genital nude?

It doesn't matter what they are, for they are not a very nice being, and that's all that really matters.

The sewing machine stops its racket, and we

CUT TO CLOSE-UP

BABY RUDOLPH

They are applying chapstick now. Centuries of Land of Christmas weather has puckered their lips up like a constipated dog's arsehole, but it is nothing that a good old rub of Carmex Cherry and Strawberry can't fix, and they apply it liberally, even though the stuff costs a fortune and they can only get it from the Elfernet in bulk.

They slap their lips together in that way women often do when applying lippy, and stares at themself in a little round mirror, one of those ones you keep in your bathroom that makes your head small on one side and makes it giant if you flip it.

"I'd fluff me," they say, whatever the fuck that means. "I'd fluff me so hard." Oh, they mean... yes, quite.

They pocket the chapstick, which is amazing, since they have no pockets, but they've definitely put it somewhere about their person for safekeeping, and it's up to you, the viewer, to imagine just where that might be. They stand up and pull from the sewing machine whatever it is they've been working studiously upon.

It is a shawl—a rather terrible one at that, for they are not too great at machine stitch-work and could have perhaps benefitted from a course showing them how to do it—and they wrap it around themself before dancing their way to the middle of the room, hips a-swinging to the music.

CUT TO CLOSEUP

Our captive, Ahora, doesn't know where to look, so she closes her eyes instead and wishes her captor would just fuck off already.

FADE OUT
ROLL LITIGATION.

BABY RUDOLPH

9

The Partridge Inn was packed to the rafters, even though it didn't have rafters; Norm had had them removed on account of them making the place look scruffy. When Finklefoot entered, saw the busyness of the place, he turned round and was half-out the door again when someone shouted his name from across the room.

Rat and Jimbo stood next to the bar; it had been Jimbo whose voice had somehow risen above the mumbling, rhubarbing extras knocking about the place in small groups.

"Ah, what the hell," Finklefoot sighed, and then veritably fought his way through the overpaid bit players to reach his two favourite workers. Which didn't say much for them, just that they were very seldom late and did manage to get a bit done on those days ending with Y.

"What's on tonight, then?" asked Finklefoot. Then to Norm, who was working on a crossword and ignoring the pleas and shouts of those with empty glasses, he said, "The usual please, Norm."

Norm dropped his pencil and set about the beer pump as if it had just said something negative about his mother; you could say what you liked about Norm, but he took care of his regulars, which was why Finklefoot was getting served and everyone else wasn't. Good old-fashioned favouritism.

"Ahora's choir. It's now Hattie Quim's choir," Jimbo said, putting his elbow in something wet and sticky. "Most of this lot are in it," he made an all-encompassing gesture to the masses, "and this is where they've decided to hold their meetings.

"That's a bit of a cunt's trick, isn't it?" said Finklefoot, for it was. "What if someone wants to just have a quiet drink? I don't want to have to listen to that old tart going on all night about octaves and falsettos, and all that nonsense."

"Don't look like we've got much choice," said Rat, necking his Scotch and signalling Norm for 'same again'. "This'll all be over in a week, once the Land of Christmas Annual Variety Show has come and gone. Then we can all go back to being useless at singing, dancing, and doing magic tricks. Speaking of which, have you—"

"If the word *Bee* or *Gees* should even pass your lips this evening, Rat, I shall not be held responsible for the kicking you will most probably receive. Do I make myself clear?"

"Crystal," said Rat, tossing a peanut up into the air and catching it in his mouth.

BABY RUDOLPH

"Good," Finklefoot said as Norm pushed a pint in his general direction, and he gratefully took it up and supped at it. "I've had a helluva day already, and I'm here to relax. Then it's off home for me to see to the beloved, brewer's droop willing, and then to sleep, where I shall no doubt suffer many nightmares and end up awakening in a pool of both sweat and piss."

He took his place on a stool at the bar and glanced about the room. He saw a lot of faces he recognised, many of them from the jigsaw factory, and just then it occurred to him that Ahora's abductor could very well be present. Any one of them—or perhaps even two or three—could be responsible for her sudden and mysterious disappearance. Like dentine after years of eating sweets and drinking tea with seven sugars, he suddenly felt very exposed.

"What's the matter with your face?" Jimbo asked as he tapped his pint on the bar in an effort to bring it back to life.

Finklefoot snapped out of it; he had been one step away from complete paranoia. "Today," he said, "The Fat Bastard put me in charge of finding Ahora, Queen of the thousand-piece puzzle."

"Find her?" Rat said with a frown. Rat always looked as if you had just asked him to find a word that rhymed with "month", but sometimes it was worse than others, and this was one of those.

"Perhaps I should start at the beginning," said Finklefoot, and he did. He explained his unceremonious summons early in the day from The Fat Bastard, and then his visit to the LCPD station house, where he'd encountered two of the least qualified officers of law you could ever imagine, and then how they had explained to him that Krampus was not, in fact, the head of the Tories on Earth, but was imprisoned beneath their feet, and had been for the past decade. At the mere mention of his name, both Rat and Shart had made the sign of the cross, and Rat had for some reason dipped dirty fingers into his Scotch and rubbed them across Finklefoot's forehead, a gesture that would, Finklefoot told him, result in a trip to the hospital should it ever occur again.

"What I don't quite get," said Jimbo, and he too had affected the expression of someone struggling to rhyme a word with "month". Bumf, maybe? The type of tedious mail, fast food menus or premature cremation services, that everyone receives. No, bumf didn't quite rhyme with month; it was the "m" that did it. That "m" stuck out like a sore thumb, and anyway, wasn't Jimbo about to say something about what he didn't quite get?

"Hm?" said Finklefoot, for Jimbo had fallen silent for some reason and was staring off, blankly, into the distance as if he'd just remembered he'd left the gas on.

"Oh, yes, right!" Jimbo said, then added, "What I don't quite get is why The Fat Bastard has felt it appropriate to enlist your help. I mean, you're not police, and the last I checked, you hadn't passed your PI badge."

Finklefoot nodded as he lit his pipe. His friend was making perfect sense, for a change, but that's the thing with friends: occasionally they will surprise you. "It's because I helped to put that big, hairy bastard behind bars all those years ago. Something about having form." That was, of course, complete nonsense. It couldn't be called form if it only happened once a decade. That was like saying Hitler hadn't killed anyone in over seventy years; he was probably a nice bloke now.

"Can we please not talk about... rhymes with strampus... anymore," said Rat, conspiratorially. "I've a funny feeling this is some ill-thought-out follow-up to the events of a decade ago, and the more we talk about it, the higher the chances we'll become main characters." And he turned, found the hidden camera, and grimaced into it. As fourth-wall breaks went, it was decent, if not a little forced. Seven out of ten.

"You're quite right," said Finklefoot. "Let's make a concerted effort to change the subject."

They each raised their glasses to that.

"Jessica Claus touched me here, here, and here," said Jimbo, sobbing softly and pointing at erogenous bits about his person.

"Oh, yes, my temporary replacement," Finklefoot said. He had had his reservations about The Fat Bastard dispatching his wife to take over the running of the main hub, thusly placing her in amongst hundreds of horny, little buggers. Of course, it was not Jessica Claus who he feared for, but the hundreds of horny, little buggers. It was like putting a lion amongst meerkats, only instead of killing the surrounding suricates, the lion fucked them. Fucked all of them. Fucked several of them dead, and at least one of them into hospital. "Did she give you too much trouble?"

"It all depends," said Jimbo, folding one leg over the other as if preparatory to a long and painful diatribe, "on your definition of trouble." He sighed, gawped off into the middle distance. "I shall never forget my brief but definitely illicit encounter with Mrs Claus. There I was, minding my business and filling the pissing dolls up with ersatz piss, when all of a sudden I felt a presence in the space behind me. My manufacturing cubicle, of course, is tall, and so I knew I was partitioned off from the rest of the factory, hidden and at the mercy of whoever it was that now made me feel incredibly nervous." He paused, shook an inordinate number of pills into his hand from a bottle, then chucked them into his mouth before crunching them up and moving on with his tale. "I turned slowly round, like a kebab on a vertical spit, and there she was, all dressed in red. Well, I say 'all dressed' but that's like saying our friend Shart is 'all there'. She was practically naked, is what I'm getting at, and her female bits and bobs were hanging all over the place. It took me longer than I care to divulge to figure out what it was I was looking at, which meant that I was just staring, open-mouthed, at her, which obviously she mistook for lust. I don't mind telling you, but not my wife, that I did have certain stirrings about the trouser area. However, as a married elf I did what any decent elf would do. I closed my eyes and thought of Granny Hoverboard." He took an almighty pull on his ale and tapped the bar, the universal sign for 'same again'. "That was when she touched me," he said, "on my ear, my nose, and then my middle nipple."

Finklefoot didn't know what a middle nipple was—euphemism, perhaps, for happy-nozzle—but he was appalled that one of his best workers should be accosted so... so brazenly, and also wondered where she would be at around nine o'clock in the morning.

"And where were you when all this was happening?" Finklefoot asked of Rat, who had gone noticeably quiet.

"I saw her come in," Rat said. "So I was hiding in the corner, already thinking about his Granny Hoverboard."

Finklefoot was about to retort when there came a sudden kerfuffle in the pub, and all eyes turned to the door, more importantly, the person who had just come through it.

"For fuck's sake," Jimbo muttered, turning his back on the newcomer as if avoiding her attention.

Hattie Quim, for it was she, was the forelady of the liquorice factory, which should have meant that she was something of a sweetie, when in fact the opposite was true. She was, for want of a better word, a cunt, one of Nature's little prototypes, if Nature had been going for a poisoned chalice of a woman. It made sense now that her husband had volunteered to be Chief of Police. He was probably already well-versed in the art of handcuff application; kicking a criminal about the floor was probably second nature to him, and he'd learnt it all from his spouse, whose temper had a tendency, like the TV remote control or that special pair of reading glasses that make the text bigger without compromising on style, to get lost for several months at a time.

The drinkers all surrounded Hattie as soon as she came through the door, and were imploring her to provide an update on something or other.

"What's all that about?" asked Finklefoot, for it seemed he was out of the loop on everything these days, and he'd only been removed from his usual activities for twelve hours, at most.

"She's offered to take over the choir for The Land of Christmas Annual Variety Show," said Jimbo, head still down on the bar. It was stuck there, in all honesty, for Norm hadn't given it a good wipe down for three hours.

"Yeah," Rat said. "Since Ahora's missing, the choir is desperate for a replacement choirmistress, and Hattie threw her, well, hat into the ring and was unanimously voted in by this lot." He made an all-encompassing gesture which almost displaced several empty pint glasses and a half-empty peanut bowl.

"Why would anyone want to sing under that... that perimenopausal menace?" said Finklefoot. At the bar, two middle-aged women turned and gave him a look that suggested he'd better shut his face. A little quieter, he said, "I mean, she'll treat them all like absolute shit from the heel of her boot."

"As that may be," said Jimbo, peeling his face from the bar with a stainless-steel fish-slice Norm had given to him, "she'll have that choir ship-shape and ready to go by the weekend. There won't be a bum note. because anyone silly enough to make one will be shown the door. You mark my words, that choir will be the best damn choir ever to perform in The Land of Christmas Annual Variety Show. They've already won it; just need the silverware to prove it." His forehead came loose, and he made a mental note not to do that again, just as Shart was staggering toward the toilet.

"Ooh, a fish-slice!" he slurred, and accepted the gift from Jimbo without breaking step. As he fell into the men's room, Finklefoot said:

"You do realise what he's going to do with that."

"As long as he don't get blood all over my urinals," Norm said, overhearing, "and he gives it a good scrub afterwards, I don't mind."

Hattie Quim arrived at the bar, ordered a large Aperol Spritz, whatever the hell that was, and turned to face the trio of elves perched there, avoiding eye-contact and whistling to themselves.

"I can *do* the drink," said Norm, "but I don't have no ice."

"No ice!" Hattie exclaimed. "And also your use of double negatives needs to be addressed, but that's not important right now." She took a step back from the bar and gave it another go, this time with gusto, "No ice! No ice! How can there be no ice? This is The Land of Christmas! I would like to speak to your manager!"

Norm didn't know what to say to that. Did he have a manager? A look to Jimbo, Rat, and then Finklefoot; their slight shakes of head suggested he was well within his rights to refuse this lady a drink, and also to bodily evict her from the pub until further notice, or such time as ice was made available to him.

"Hattie," he said. "I am the manager of this est-hablish-a-ment, as you well know, so pipe down and I'll make your silly little cocktail, without ice, but if you continue to make s scene, well..." He turned to Rat, Jimbo, and Finklefoot.

They shook their heads again, even more slightly this time. It meant, D*on't threaten her or she'll have her husband come and arrest you.* Luckily, Norm interpreted it correctly.

"... would you like it in a balloon glass, or a small shoe?"

Hattie told him 'the shoe', and watched closely as he set about making it. She didn't want to be drinking from a *dirty* shoe, after all. As she continued to watch—*supervise*, in fact, as watching didn't usually require a notebook and pen—and without taking her eyes off Norm and his mixology skills, of which he had zero but you could always rely on him for a 'the usual' or 'same again', Hattie said:

"I take it you three'll be competing at the show." It was neither a question nor a statement; it was amazing how she could do that. And also annoying as fuck.

Now, something happened in the next three seconds that, if you were to ask him later, Finklefoot would recount, with great regret, just what the hell came over him. First, he took in the ambience of the pub, saw that it was filled with members of Hattie Quim's choir, and worked himself up to a frenzied One on the madness scale. Secondly, he thought about said choir holding that trophy, all bristling with energy and with smug smiles about their countenances that a good man would take immense pleasure in wiping off with a swift backhanded slap, and he moved up to Two. Thirdly, and the thing that made him do something he would spend the next week regretting with every fibre of his being, was Hattie's stupid head and the way it sat on top of a stupid body, and no one thought to mention it to her, or call her out on her bullshit, so that was level Three of an imagined scale in which his blood was boiling and his head wasn't working quite right. Which led to this. In slow motion. With a multitude of cameras, so that he could watch it back over and over and over again, mainly at night when he was trying to fall asleep.

"We're doing the *Bee Gees!*" said Finklefoot, much to the surprise of Rat and Jimbo, who now wore the expressions of elves who had just been informed of a substantial lottery win with a ticket neither of them had purchased and that had gone through the wash three times and was now nothing more than a brittle, white piece of paper whose numbers could just be made out, if you looked really hard and were willing to forgive the missing barcode.

"The *Bee Gees?*" Hattie said. She had her drink now and was sucking it up through a straw pushed into one of her receptacle's shoelace holes. "You three? The *Bee Gees?*" And then she did laugh, and it was rather loud. Eyes fell upon them from all around the bar. Finklefoot gave these eyes two fingers.

"That's right!" Rat said, grinning like a cat who'd not only got the cream, but was making a lovely gateau with it, too. "You are looking at the future winners of The Land of

Christmas Annual Variety Show," and then added, "No autographs, please, we're very humble over here on the winning side of the bar."

Behind the bar, Norm drew back the pencil and small bit of paper he had thrust in their direction, then muttered something grimly about how he hated when people let fame go to their heads.

"It's *good* to have dreams," Hattie said, counting change out of her purse and stacking it neatly on the bar like an OCD architect. "However, I'm afraid you've picked the wrong year to compete. Ahora's choir, Santa rest her soul, now *my* choir, will be impossible to beat. You're on to a hiding to nothing; once I mould this little lot into worthy winners, you'll wish you'd never been born."

"I already do," said Finklefoot. "And if I ever find out who my parents are, I shall sue them within an inch of their inconsiderate lives, but that's not the point." And it wasn't, for he had something on his mind that would perhaps be better if he said it aloud. "When was the last time YOU saw Ahora of the jigsaw factory, Mrs Quim?" A simple Hattie would have done, he supposed, but fuck it. He was in detective mode, and detectives use respectful honorifics, if nothing else but to throw their suspects off.

BABY RUDOLPH

Hattie Quim's face dropped, and it took her a few seconds to pick it up off the floor. "And what is *that* supposed to mean?" she asked. "Are you suggesting *I* know something about her disappearance. Or, the lord he bendeth me over and giveth me a jolly good spanking, you think I had *something to do* with it."

"I never said that," Finklefoot said. However, he was enjoying what Hattie Quim was doing with her face right now as indignance and unmitigated rage fought for supremacy, leaving her looking as though she was sucking on a sour wasp.

"How dare you insinuate that *I* had anything at all to do with the disappearance of Ahora Whorer," Hattie said in a stage whisper. It was unclear at this point whether she wanted an audience or not.

"Ahora Whorer?" Jimbo said.

"Is that her full name?" Rat added, turning it over in his mouth. "Ahora Whorer... Ahora Whorer... I like the way it sounds. It tickles the tongue, if you do it properly."

"I'm just saying," said Finklefoot, "that it's a little convenient that she's gone missing a week before the variety show, leaving the way clear for you to snap up her choir, mould them into your own, and win the goddamn whole thing for yourself." When put like that, it was obviously Hattie Quim whodunnit. But Finklefoot was nothing if not professional, and would wait for a scrap of evidence to land in his lap.

And it would.

"I've never been so insulted in my life!" said Hattie.

"Really?" said Rat. "That does surprise me."

That did it for Mrs Quim; the straw that broke the camel's back, and then drove the camel to a hospital where they didn't accept "his sort's" insurance. And with one final huff, Hattie took up her drink, spun around at least one, and marched away, where she was swamped by excitable choristers.

"Hm," Finklefoot said.

A moment later, Shart came out of the toilets with a fish-slice stuck in his back. Quite how it had got there was anyone's guess.

BABY RUDOLPH

10

The first rule of Secret Comedy Club is that you tell everyone about it, and they tell their friends, and them theirs, and then, invariably, everyone decides they have something better to do on that particular evening and so don't bother turning up to the bloody thing, which "Probably wouldn't have been much cop, anyway, as the comedians were all up-and-comers," which usually meant they stole their material from better-known comics and hoped no one noticed.

This was Rudolph's first time and, peering through the satin red curtains as people took their seats and opened bags of sweets, his bumhole did twitchings and he had a good mind to locate the club's promoter and ask why he had saw it fit to put Rudolph at the foot of the bill, where surely it would be bettered suited for someone with more experience.

Backstage was bristling with activity; that is to say, the three comedians performing after him ran through their jokes and stole ones from those within earshot.

Rudolph was scared.

He was tired.

And he was still thinking about Merthyr Titful and her social media of horror. He just couldn't shake it from his thoughts, or what he was going to do about it, but it seemed he had very few options and was fairly screwed whatever he did.

Ignoring her was a possibility, but that would only last until he was face-to-face with her once again. Then he would have some explaining to do, and would no doubt buckle under pressure, tell her he was sorry, and end up proposing.

Another of his unappealing options was to tell someone he trusted, and hope that by the time they stopped laughing, they found it within their hearts to at least sympathise with him, and offer him some sort of advice moving forward.

A final option was to kill Merthyr and then himself. He tried not to think about that one too much.

"On in five, Rudy," said a voice. Rudolph turned to find that the voice had fallen from a face he recognised.

"Okay, thanks," Rudolph told Dorman, the club's promoter and the elf who'd given him this chance to hone his skills before the variety show. Dorman had a clipboard and was perusing it the way one might a menu at a posh restaurant. Tonight's special, Rudolph thought, was pan-fried embarrassment in an anxiety sauce, with regret croutons on the side, served on a bed of wish-I'd-stayed-in-bed, and finished with a dressing of Oh, well, you learn from your mistakes.

The audience were all muttering amongst themselves and chewing toffees. The aforementioned "On in five" turned to four and three, and then two minutes, and after about twenty more minutes, or so it seemed, ticked over to one. Rudolph was stood behind the curtain wondering if it was too late to change his mind when there came an amplified squawk and then Dorman's voice, or something like it, began to speak.

"Ladies and gentlemen, elves and elflings, welcome to another evening of raucous comedy. Before we begin, I'd like to remind you that photographs are okay, but filming with mobile phones is, like sleeping with your sister, strictly forbidden." This got a little laugh, but also a groan for those amongst the audience who had no problem at all with a little bit of "Keeping it in the family", because incest was an anagram of nicest, and you couldn't argue with that. Or something.

"Tonight we have for you Terry "Totally Twatty" Tibbins." He paused there to accommodate an applause that came eventually, though when it did it was the clap for the final runner in a marathon to cross the finish line. Usually an octogenarian or some fella with robot legs. "We have The Brothers Blimp, we have Callie Broccoli, but first up, I want you to give this guy a very warm welcome. It's his first time on stage, and will not be his last, probably. Please, put your hands and hooves together for Rudolph!"

The applause started.

Right, so that was all done and, Rudolph thought, done rather well, but what happened next was that the curtains didn't fly open, the way he thought they might, and so he stood there like an idiot with his face pushed into crushed satin until Dorman came along and told him the curtains were broken and you had to just fight with them for a bit until you found yourself on the stage.

"Ah!" said Rudolph, and began kicking the heavy curtains this way and that and headbutting the bits his hooves missed. He didn't so much as saunter onto the stage, but it certainly wasn't how he'd planned it.

No sooner had he appeared to the crowd than the applause suddenly stopped, making way for a deafening silence, and a drunken voice from the back said, "Say sumfin funny then!"

"It's, uh, erm, it's really nice to, um, be here," said Rudolph, battling with a stool and a microphone until he had them just where he wanted them. He talked as he worried away at the stage accoutrements, but none of what he was saying was relevant, nor was it funny. It was filler of the worst kind. "Anyone here from Dallas?" and that sort of thing. No one was from Dallas, of course, since Dallas was in an adjacent dimension, but Rudolph had to do *something* about the anxious nothingness he could hear from the audience. After a whole minute of microphone adjusting, stool placement, microphone readjusting—he'd set it for standing in the first instance—stool replacement, since one of the legs had dropped off the first one, Rudolph settled himself down onto the edge of the stool and, for the first time, looked out into the audience. He saw...

Not much, really, on account of there being a bloody great white light in his face. For a moment, he thought he'd passed on, and looked about the place in search of heavenly relatives. A heckle of, "Come on, you antler bastard! I've had to get a babysitter for this, and I'm buggered if she's getting overtime, ya prick!" brought him back into the room.

And so Rudolph began his set in earnest, starting off with a tester for the audience, to see if they were willing to accept the rude stuff. "Why was The Fat Bastard pissed off when he got a sweater for Christmas?"

Suitable pause.

Quick glance about the place.

And onto the punchline.

"Because," said Rudolph with a smile, "he'd asked for a squirter instead."

One laugh.

One more.

A third.

"Okay, yeah," said Rudolph, satisfied with the reaction. "We're gonna have a good time, I can tell," said he. "Right. What's next? Um… Why are Christmas trees fucking shit at knitting?… Too many needles, that's right. What's worse than Mommy kissing Santa Claus?… Daddy giving me a reacharound. Did you guys hear about the Grinch? Yeah, he took Viagra… grew three inches that day. What's worse than an elf on a shelf?… A hoe on her flow."

It went on for almost five minutes without too much fuss, and the deeper into his set he got, the more Rudolph relaxed. He even, at one point, lit a cigarette and began swishing a glass of Sherry round, the way clever, smug, over-confident comics invariably do just before a sudden downfall, and it wasn't too long before Rudolph fell down with, what he thought, was a relatively harmless gag.

BABY RUDOLPH

"So, what do you call it when a dozen elves run a train on Jessica Claus?" He paused, as always, allowing time for someone in the crowd to shout out the answer, although it had never occurred to him what he would do if that actually happened, such was his comedy naivety. It would fairly fuck up the rest of the show. Fortunately, once again no one replied. With no small amount of relief, Rudolph said, "The Polar Express!"

And it was *that* that did it.

A half-filled (hopefully ale, probably piss) plastic cup slammed into the side of Rudolph's face, and he made a *gnh!* sound, which he hadn't made for quite some time, especially not with an exclamation mark.

"You suck!" opined one voice.

"I lost my husband to that bitch!" screamed another.

"Anyone got any rotten fruit?" enquired a third.

"Just plums," a fourth helpfully replied.

"That'll do," said the third voice again.

And then Rudolph was pelted with plump, purple plums, which really annoyed him because, if there was one thing he hated more than being cancelled mid-gig, it was alliteration.

He fell off his stool and was about to make a dart for the curtains—Dorman's head was peering through, and he looked concerned, and also angry—when something miraculous happened, something which changed the course of the evening, and also the rest of his life.

"Leave him alone, ya wee fannies!" bellowed a voice. It was one that Rudolph immediately recognised. But he hadn't seen her come in. Had she been there all along? She might very well have been; a three-hundred-watt bulb had prevented Rudolph from seeing anything except the red nose on his own stupid face.

No sooner had the voice spoken than the whole audience piped down. There were murmurs, whispers, and confused gibberings, as the crowd tried to figure out what to do next.

"Is there," Rudolph said, "any chance I can have the house lights up for a moment?" He waited, heart beating frantically within, and thought, *I'm probably never gonna get invited back after this.*

The house lights were nothing special, not expensive theatre lights that you can dim up or down, change the colour of, make flash to annoy the epileptics, synchronise with music and all that unnecessary guff.

BABY RUDOLPH

At the edge of the room, Callie Broccoli flicked a switch and the lights came on. It was like that moment after a good night's drinking and dancing when, with no consideration at all, someone just decides enough is enough and floods the room with light, and you find out you've been dancing with an absolute cactus of a woman all night long.

Just like that, this was.

"That's right!" said Merthyr, for it was she, and she did not look happy with the elves and reindeer all around her. "He might not be the funniest fucker in the land," she went on, "or even this room, but he's funny, so give him a break, or I'll have nae choice but to put ma hoof through ya. Capisce?"

Rudolph watched from the stage and suddenly wished it was one of those ones with a trapdoor, and that the trapdoor had been known to malfunction, and that it would now suddenly open and drop him down into the abyss. That sort of feeling.

"Now," said Merthyr, returning to her knitting—what looked like a tartan scarf—and still shaking her head with annoyance. "Who wants to hear me sing? I know all sorts: Shaggy, Snow, Limp Bizkit, all sorts…"

It was unanimously decided that Merthyr should give them a bit of *Informer* by Snow, so she did.

"Informer, ya no say daddy me Snow me I go blame. I licky boom boom down," she went as she knitted. To say you had to be there to thoroughly understand how powerful this performance was, was an understatement. When she was done—six verses and at least eight choruses—she put her knitting away in her handbag and said:

"Now, mah babeh Rudy is gonna finish his bit, and yous are gonna laugh, ya wee bald monkeys, and nae more interruptions. Sent from Elf Fon."

Complete silence had once again fallen upon the room as they all, as a collective, tried to figure out what "Sent from Elf Fon" meant. and also why this big fat reindeer was speaking in what appeared to be tongues, but was, unbeknownst to them, perfect Scottish.

It was decided, silently and by a combination of shrugs and raised eyebrows alone, that they would behave themselves as an audience, if only because she was much bigger than them and appeared to be a direct descendant of William Wallace, whoever that was.

"Right... um, I've only got a few jokes to go," said Rudolph as the lights came down (flicked off) again, "so bear with me, and I'll... um, I'll be out of your hair."

BABY RUDOLPH

The rest of his set went without incident, though it was impossible to tell whether the laughter was genuine, now, or if the audience was putting it on in an effort to evade Merthyr's wrath. Still, Rudolph thought, fake laughter was better than no laughter. You only had to ask James Corden to know that.

"Thank you!" Rudolph said, bowing his head a few times. "You've all been great!" He backed toward the red curtain. The audience applauded, mumbled, and cheered falsely, but above all the noise, which wasn't quite enough to raise the rafters, but wasn't far off, Rudolph could hear one laugh in particular.

That of Merthyr, the colossal, bad-breathed, sweary, unhinged reindeer who might have just saved his career from ending before it had even got off the ground whilst simultaneously frightening the shit out of him and everyone else in the room, including the doormen.

"Hahahahaha!" she went. And, "Ahhahahaha, ya funny wee bastard, ye!"

When Rudolph got backstage, he was already holding back tears. When he accidentally stubbed his dewclaw on someone's ill-stored guitar case, the match in the powder barrel, he was weeping like a baby with sunburn.

Maybe, like James Corden, comedy was just not for him, but one thing he had never expected was to garner the attention of a hulking superfan, and not only that, but one who was talking all manner of nonsense on the Elfernet. He didn't know what was worse: that his first night at Secret Comedy Club had gone so terribly, that he still had Saturday's performance in The Land of Christmas Annual Variety Show to come, or the fact that he was probably going to wake up one of these days next to the decapitated head of one of his friends.

It didn't bear thinking about, so Rudolph, for the second time that day, made a run for it.

On the flight home, he clipped two pigeons in what could only be described as a hit-and-run.

He cried himself to sleep that night, and suffered awful dreams in which an audience of bandaged birds cawed and heckled and threw seed at him until he promised to stop telling jokes.

Merthyr, thankfully, did not make an appearance in his nightmares.

Perhaps because she was too busy giving Freddy Krueger bad dreams.

11

Finklefoot was drunk by the time Norm started covering the pumps with filthy towels. It had been a lively night, inasmuch as Rat, Jimbo, and Finklefoot had pretty much finished off a bottle of Scotch between them, and had even moved on to Jaegerbombs, some new-fangled creation of Norm's that was enough to knock even the most seasoned of alcoholics off their feet and onto their heads.

There is, Finklefoot slurred in his mind, *not a chance of my beloved getting any action tonight.* And he was right. No amount of Viagra could revive his poor pecker, and even if it did, he wouldn't know what to do with it. Probably, he thought, end up trying to put up those shelves she keeps going on about with it. Or taking photos of it to send to all the girls in his contact list. They love it when elf-men do that, especially if they'd said, "Fuck off, perv!" the first three times.

"In the words of Winston Churchill," said Norm to the stragglers lying about the place in steaming piles, "'Piss of home!'"

"I believe," said Finklefoot, pulling himself up from the floor, where he'd made something of a comfortable bed from the unconscious bodies of Rat and Jimbo, "that was Gandhi!"

"Did we pass out?" Rat enquired as he, too, propelled himself slowly up and into the vertical plane. "I fear that new concoction of yours shall be used for Machiavellian purposes, Norm," he slurred and rubbed at his temples. "I'd best be off home to the missus," he added as an afterthought.

"That might prove fruitless," Jimbo said, joining his cohorts in the standing position. "You don't have a missus."

"Ah," went Rat. "'Tis very true. Then perhaps it is not too late to find one daft enough to accompany me home, where sweet love will be attempted, and many promises of a call-back will ensue, and neither of which will happen, so what's the point?" He sighed plaintively; a peanut fell from his left nostril.

"What happened to the choir?" Finklefoot asked of the barman as he searched the place for signs of life. "I thought they'd be in for the night."

Norm whipped a filthy towel from his shoulder and began rubbing at the bar with it. So sticky was that bar that he had to use the fish-slice to rescue the filthy towel. "They all pissed off about twenty minutes ago," he said, grunting as he worked.

"And Hattie?" Finklefoot said.

"She's only just left," Norm said, emptying half-filled (half-empty, if you were one of those miserable folks) bowls of peanuts back into the gigantic wholesale sack he kept them in at night. Rodents loved those nuts. They wouldn't if they realised how out of date they were. Some of those nuts had seen the second coming of Santa.

"Just?" said Finklefoot, quickly sobering up. "As in, most recently?"

Norm nodded. "Yeah, *just*," he said, as if the word was made from razorblades and he was an ex-cutter. "She stepped over you lot to get to her umbrella."

Finklefoot was fully sober again now; there was a good chance his beloved, Trixie, would get three seconds of immense pleasure, *after* all. But not before...

"I must be off, fellas," Finklefoot said. "Duty calls, and all that."

"Are we still going to learn 'New York Mining Disaster 1941' tomorrow night?" Rat called after him, but Finklefoot was out the door and into the snowy night before you could say: Potential elfnapper on the move. Over.

Finklefoot said it anyway.

*

It was below freezing outside, and the snow wasn't so much as pissing down, but rather slicing the air like millions of tiny guillotines. It was that kind of snow that whips off your ears as if it knows how much it hurts and takes magnificent pleasure in doing it.

Practising sadist, this snow was, and as Finklefoot pushed through it, he could have sworn he heard the individual snowflakes screaming out their joyful, barbarous orgasms as they assaulted his uncovered bits. "You like that, you dirty little bitch!" said one flake as it exploded against his left lobe. "Take it, slut!" said another as it skimmed off the helix of his right ear. He was about to tell them to shut up their noise when he remembered he was stealthily following someone, and settled for pulling his hat down to one side, so that only one of his ears was exposed instead. It was like choosing which of the twins was your favourite, and leaving the other one to, well, get sexually assaulted by the snow.

In the words of Billy Pilgrim, *So it goes.*

And it does.

BABY RUDOLPH

Finklefoot had located, amongst the copious prints in the snow, those belonging to Harrie Quim. And how did he know they were hers? Well, the others were moving in a straight line and slightly faded, as in half-filled with fresh snow.

Hattie Quim was staggering.

Finklefoot was almost sick in his mouth and quickly rephrased it.

She was all over the shop, was Hattie Quim, the detrimental results of eight Aperol Spritz, no doubt, and so it was a relatively simple task to not lose her, for her prints were clear, new, and made by feet which didn't know whether they were coming or going, which was probably why Finklefoot had spent the first ten minutes going in circles.

Finklefoot did not know where Hattie Quim called home, but he had an inkling it was in one of the more affluent areas of the land. Her job as forelady of the liquorice factory had probably afforded her one or two benefits which those beneath her would never receive. Nice house. Government-funded outdoor decorations. Twice-weekly bin collection. One of those welcome mats that says "There is no reason for you to be here" on it in an annoying, cursive font. Yes, Finklefoot had her number, for it was one he was familiar with. As the foreman of the main hub, he too was able to put his bins out twice a week, and although his welcome mat says, "Can't you just text me?" they were one and the same.

He gagged again.

"Bloody hell," he said, wiping drool from his chin before resuming his quest to follow her. There was, he reminded himself, someone's life on the line, and if he didn't find Ahora soon, before she showed up dead, as the police liked to put it, then the chances of her being dead by the time she showed up were unfathomable. It would all make sense come morning-time, Finklefoot reminded himself.

"What the bloody hell are you doing here?" a voice screeched.

Finklefoot looked up for the first time in about ten minutes and, through a mist of falling snow, saw that he was standing in an alleyway, and that Hattie Quim was also there, only she was in a crouching position with her knickers round her ankles. The snow all around her was beginning to turn yellow.

"Do you mind?" she screeched, perhaps feeling a little self-conscious and humiliated. As if to prove that, yes, she was both of those things, she gave her lettuce a quick shake and pulled her knickers up.

BABY RUDOLPH

Finklefoot stopped whistling and pretending there was something worth looking at on the wall to his right, but only when Hattie Quim started accusing him of all sorts of terrible things did he think it best he defended himself.

"Why have you followed me all the way from the pub?" she asked. "A rapist, are you? Just a dirty old rapist about to take advantage of a half-pissed woman elf? I'll scream." She took from her purse a small tubular thingy, and pointed it at him. "Pepper spray," she said. "Because even in The Land of Christmas, men like you exist."

"Men like... men like me," Finklefoot said, in that way that men like him did. "I'm a happily married man, Mrs Quim, and the last thing I would like is to see any harm come to you."

That was, for all intents and purposes, a bit of a lie. Nothing *bad*, of course, but if something should fall upon her—a small piano, perhaps, or an anvil—then who was he to stand in the way.

"Then why did you follow me into this alleyway?" she said, glancing about the place and then grimacing, as if she didn't like what she saw. "When you live on the other side of town, why have you followed me all the way from the pub to this alleyway?" She took something else from her purse and pushed the button that made a small bolt of lightning dance between its electrodes.

"Mrs Quim!" said Finklefoot, and it *was* Mrs Quim now, and not Hattie, for she had a bloody taser and was threatening him with it. He acted accordingly by throwing his hands into the air and breaking wind. "I can assure you that I was simply making sure that you got home safely," he said, which wasn't bad considering he'd just now come up with it. "I was, how can I put this without you turning me into a deep-fried little person... I was merely walking you to your door without you knowing I was, in fact, walking you to your door."

This seemed to enrage Hattie Quim further, and the voltage of her taser seemed to turn itself up.

"That's ridiculous!" she said. "Do I look like the kind of lady that needs a bodyguard after dark?"

"You look ridiculously well prepared," said Finklefoot, "and do not require my services, after all." He lowered his hands, but not his heart-rate, and said, "So, I'll bid you a good evening," and turned to leave.

"I shall tell everyone about this," she said. "And that wife of yours, Trixie, she'll know what a pervert you are."

BABY RUDOLPH

That was it. Finklefoot had had enough, for he was not one of *those* men, he had not followed her into that alleyway to do unthinkable things to her, he was a good man with a beautiful wife, and he was simply trying to get to the bottom of a terrible crime, of which Hattie Quim may or may not be a part of.

"I'll tell everyone," said Finklefoot, already feeling badly about it, "that I found you in an alleyway with your knickers around your ankles, pissing. Not a terribly good look for a woman of your standing, is it? Mrs Quim, urinating in public. Federal offence, that is. I shall have to have words with that husband of yours. After all, who better to hear that is wife is a serial alley pisser than her husband, the Chief of Police?" Finklefoot said all of this without even turning to face her, but he imagined she had a right face on her. A veritable scowler of a face. An angry bastard of a—

"We'll call it quits," said Hattie.

"Goodnight, Mrs Quim!" said Finklefoot, jollily, and he took his leave of the dark alleyway and whistled as he went.

Whew, he thought, which was silly because there were dozens of good words he could have thought instead.

*

Rudolph awakened to the sound of silence, which was strange since he could have sworn he'd turned off his *The Best of Simon and Garfunkel* CD before bedding down for the night. He switched it off, and went to his computer, whose monitor was faintly flashing red every couple of seconds, which told him that there had been activity on his MyFace account, and suddenly, a cold chill engulfed him.

No, he frantically thought. *Please, no.*

Once he managed to get his hoof to do what he told it, he navigated to the notifications panel to find over a hundred new ones awaiting his approval.

"What in the name of love...?"

He clicked the Notifications tab and was redirected to a page that consisted of dozens and dozens of pictures of him at various stages of his performance at the Secret Comedy Club the previous night: here he was struggling to get the microphone at the right height; there he was falling off his stool; here he was looking terrified, a deer in the headlights, in front of the audience; there he was apologising to them for his over-usage of the "C" word. One after another, picture, picture, picture, and all shot from what must have been Merthyr's place in the crowd. Each photograph was accompanied by some inane comment from Merthyr, all of which were signed off with Sent from Elf-Fon, Snet form E-Fun, Snot for Elfin, or some derivative. There were more pictures here than Rudolph had ever seen taken of one unique event; even the arraignment of Krampus hadn't been this well-covered.

Yet it wasn't the terrifying number of photographs of the event that sent ice-needles down his spine, nor the way in which she referred to him as "my Rudy" or "ma babeh Rudolph" in her attached comments, although that was certainly enough to turn his blood to mercury.

There was a private message; a DM, if you know what's what, or a computer text if you haven't got a clue. Just one message sitting idly in his inbox, dormant, lying in wait, the way a man might wait for a woman in a dark alley only to find out that she's just a serial pisser, and not in fact an elfnapper. That sort of thing.

A single message that looked at him from the corner of the screen and winked and said, *I dare you.*

Rudolph simply stared back at it. *Two can play at that game*, he thought, since it was better than, *I can stare harder than you.* But there was only so much of that he could take, and decided that the only way he was going to find out what it said—he already knew its sender, that was a given—and make it stop looking at him as if he was dessert was to click on it.

He clicked on it.

Merthyr's huge face filled the left of the screen, and on the right it said:

Picnic tomorrow. Candycane Park, Noon. Dinnae keep me waitin, babeh Rudy!
SNT FROM ELF-FOON

The stable was suddenly even colder, somehow, and Rudolph went, "Gnnn," through gritted teeth and visibly shook like a shitting Pomeranian. For the longest time—seven minutes and thirty-six seconds—Rudolph just stared at the message as if it had just called his dead mother a good lay. You couldn't put into words just how he felt in that moment, even if you were an infinite number of monkeys with access to an infinite number of typewriters, which just went to show that you can lead a simian to a Smith Corona, but you can never get the bloody things to do as their told.

Such were monkeys.

Dinnae keep me waitin?

BABY RUDOLPH

What did that even mean? It took Rudolph several attempts on paper and about twenty out loud, and it was only when he accidentally dislocated his jaw that it made sense.

Don't keep me waiting.

She spoke and typed English, but in an extraordinary way.

Such were Scotsmen.

But Rudolph, of course, did not know what a Scotsman looked like, let alone sounded like, so a mooter point had never been made, and suchlike.

A picnic suggestion, Rudolph guessed, sounded nice when it was from a friend or a female partner you shared feelings with, but this was not a suggestion, nor was it from someone Rudolph loved, or even liked.

Feared.

Yes, he certainly feared Merthyr, and from what he had seen so far, with good reason. She was clearly battling with some things mentally, a polite way of saying she was a fucking nutter and this picnic was the one sandwich of which she was short.

Rudolph, after almost an hour of mulling it over, decided to reply, and tell her *exactly* what he thought of her picnic idea. "Sounds great," said his message. And also, "Wouldn't miss it for the world." Quite why he had done that, he didn't know, but it had something to do with self-preservation, and keeping enemies closer than friends.

It was only after he had hit Send that he realised what he had done, and what had to be done next. First, he would have to come up with some excuse to tell his trainer that would explain his absence from the Rink, then he would have to traipse halfway across the land to Candycane Park and survive a sandwich and cake lunch with a creature who, by the looks of her, was not fond of sharing food. And if he made it that far, he would have to explain to her that there was no future for them, that they simply weren't compatible, and please don't hit me.

Sleep was not forthcoming the rest of that night.

Rudolph watched reruns of *Eastenders* and sobbed quietly.

12

The Fat Bastard's office needed a serious tidy. How had he allowed it to get this bad? Everywhere he looked there were boxes of documents—it's amazing how much space two-thousand years' worth of Good or Naughty lists took up—and loose papers and bills fluttered about the place as if they were butterflies and this was their arboretum. He had tried to have it all digitised back in the late nineties, but the technology had been new, and the person who he'd paid to do it had turned out to be a hacker whose specialty was extortion. It had cost Santa almost half his fortune to keep quiet the fact that he sometimes, not always, treated himself to something kinky from Bumlove.com, and had the receipts to prove it, or *would* have them if a malicious blackmailer didn't. He could, he later realised, have blamed it all on his wife when the news inevitably broke, and no one would have been surprised by that, but hindsight is a wonderful thing, and of no dratted use to him now.

"Darling," said Santa. "Could you not do that while I'm working. And also, it's not even nine yet. In the morning. On a Tuesday. Who does... that thing, whatever it's called, on a Tuesday morning before nine? I mean, I'm all for freedom of expression, but, oh, darling, please don't wipe yourself off on the cat. That's most inappropriate, and frankly unacceptable behaviour. I shall have to give the poor thing a bath, now, and... come back here when I'm talking to... oh, she's fucked off."

All alone in the office, The Fat Bastard began to put things back in order. He had been doing so for approximately seven seconds when there came a knock at the door. And very welcome it was, too.

"Come!"

The door opened, creaked, shut, and the elf standing there said, "Any news on Ahora?"

"Finklefoot," said Father Christmas, pushing himself up from his knees, where he had been giving serious attention to a gas bill from nineteen-eighty-two. "I specifically ascribed that task to *you*."

"You *did*, and I'm working on it as we speak—"

"No, you're not," said Santa, for he was a tricksy cunt when it came to words and the veracity thereof.

"Well, not at this specific—"

"Yes, yes, never mind," said The Fat Bastard. "Tell me what you have so far, and you can leave out all the boring bits. As you can see—" He made an all-encompassing gesture. "— I've got a lot to be getting on with."

"Sir, have you ever thought about getting someone in to do it for you?"

The look he shot Finklefoot was intense enough to toast a marshmallow. As Finklefoot was just an elf, he said, "Ouch," and took a few steps backwards.

"You were telling me how you were getting on with the case," said Santa.

"Yes, quite, well," said Finklefoot, "I have my theories and shall be following them up, but Sir, is it absolutely necessary for me to be away from the factory all day? I fear for my workers."

"Jessica is taking care of them," boomed The Heavy One.

"Yes, I know," said Finklefoot, and he did. "But I'm sure that you will find, when the quarterly results come in three months from now, that they will show a sudden slump in productivity, an increase in unsanctioned toilet breaks, and a sudden surge in absences due to STI clinic appointments, and all of it will coincide with this period now, while I'm not there."

"And how do you know this?"

"Just call it a hunch, Boss," said Finklefoot.

"No," said Santa. "I don't care. I need you to track down that elfnapper, rescue Ahora, and save the day once again. For morale, if nothing else."

Finklefoot nodded and sighed. Had he thought this would go any other way? "And if she turns up dead?" he said.

"Then there's very little we can do but know that we did everything we could to find her, and it's not our fault she didn't hold on for long enough to be rescued."

Rather bleak, Finklefoot thought, but then again, The Fat Bastard had never, for as long as he'd known him, been a cheerful sort. That was all for show, for the humans. Something to do with likeability, and how jollity made all the difference between a visit from Santa and an actual home invasion.

"Then I need an assistant," Finklefoot said, for if he was going down, by God he was taking someone with him. "A Watson to my Sherlock, as it were."

"A whatnow to a whofuck?" said Santa, for he was not much of a reader. He'd given up on *To Kill a Mockingbird* when he'd discovered that no birds were even injured, let alone murdered. That was perhaps when his disillusionment with human literature had begun. It was only further exacerbated when someone told him, years later, that Atticus Finch shoots a rabid dog, and thus a better title would have been *To Kill a Rabid Dog*, silly humans.

"I would like Jimbo to assist me in my investigations," Finklefoot said, for he had not been privy to all that nonsense about Atticus Finch in The Fat Bastard's head.

Santa thought about this for a moment, stroking his beard with one hand and filling his pipe with the other. "I've already lost you, Ahora, and the entire jigsaw factory, I can scarcely afford to lose another good worker."

"That's a pity," Finklefoot said. "And just when I'm this close—" he lifted his little, three-fingered hand and set two fingers about an inch apart "—from locating Ahora, capturing the elfnapper, and putting this whole sordid affair behind us."

The Fat Bastard looked at the little, three-fingered hand and thought, Are they all like that, or has this one had a bit of a tussle with one of the machines? "Fine!" he suddenly said. "You can have Jimbo to help, but I want results, goddammit!

I want that jigsaw factory back up and running, with or without a dead Ahora to go with it."

There was a flaw in that sentence somewhere, but for the life of him Finklefoot couldn't find it.

"And Finklefoot?" said Santa to the elf who was already halfway toward the door.

"Yes?"

"You don't know anyone you trust who's also good at Excel, do you?"

*

It was a nice morning for flying, Rudolph thought. Snowing, of course, but the winds were accommodating, and the pigeons were giving him a wide berth. It was a pity, then, that he was probably heading to his own doom.

This is how naughty humans on Death Row feel, he thought as he manoeuvred his way round a church spire, when their final meal lies heavy on their stomach and the keys jangle just outside the cell door. The Green Mile, they call that final walk, so what was this?

The White Six Kilometres? Rudolph thought, though it didn't have quite the same ring to it.

BABY RUDOLPH

He was, of course, being melodramatic, and as long as he remembered his p's and q's, this would be nothing more than a pleasant picnic with beautiful surroundings, and a huge, veritable hot-air balloon of a fatty who wanted to rape, kill, and then eat him.

"Stop it!" he chastised himself. A passing swallow gave him a funny look. "She's probably nice once you get to know her, and she did save your life last night at the comedy club."

Yes, there was no getting away from the fact that she had been there and *had* had his back when things had taken a turn for the worse. That crowd was about to pepper him with rotten fruit; had it not been for Merthyr, he would have finished the night looking like something Giuseppe Arcimboldo had done between masterpieces.

"Get to know her," Rudolph said between long, deep breaths.

And you should know *better*, he reminded himself, than to bully someone based on their appearance. You have a massive red nose, you fucking weirdo! Just because she's a bit overweight and speaks in tongues, and stalks you on the socials, and sends you threatening messages in the dead of night—

"And watches you while you sleep," said a passing thrush.

"Wha—?"

But the thrush was too quick and had gone, and probably hadn't said that last bit at all.

No, the order of the day was second chances. He would spend time with Merthyr, get to know a little more about her—her hobbies, her favourite music, which Spice Girl she was and why?—and then, if his feelings remained the same as they currently were, he would tell her, *No hard feelings, but you're fucked up and I'm not looking for anything serious right now.*

She'd like that. She'd appreciate his honesty.

She'd fucking squash you, mate, and make no mistake about it.

Rudolph took a right at a thick, grey cloud and was about to empty himself one last time before he got there when a voice said:

"Rudy? It *is* you!" And then there was Cupid, flying alongside him, looking somewhat intrigued. "Where you off to, buddy? The Rinks are that way." He motioned 'that way' with his head. "Don't tell me you're skiving. You are, aren't you? Throwing a sickie?"

BABY RUDOLPH

Rudolph thought back to earlier that morning, when he'd informed his instructor by email that he wouldn't be in, on account of a gypy leg.

"Gypy leg," he said to Cupid.

Cupid looked down at it and frowned. "Seems to be doing alright to me," he said. "Probably a little out of sync with the other three, but apart from that—"

"And a virus!" Rudolph blurted. "A pretty bad virus on top of the gypy leg. Very contagious; I'd keep my distance, if I were you."

"So, you thought you'd pop out for a little fly around with a highly contagious virus, therefore making something that's already airborne even more so?" Cupid had affected the look of someone who'd just had his back pissed down, by an elf swearing blind it was just the rain.

"I thought it'd be better if I came up here, you know?" *Shut up, Rudy, you're fucking making it worse.* "There're fewer creatures up here to infect, you see. Makes some sort of sense, doesn't it? Please?"

"I'm sure it makes sense in your head," Cupid said, "if your head is all stuffed up with some sort of virus, but what about the birds? The poor birds?"

"He don't care about us," said a passing zebra finch.

"Cunt!" added its wife.

It always surprised Rudolph how all the animals in the Land of Christmas could talk; it often shocked him when they came out with stuff that would make a sailor blush.

He faked a sneeze.

"Ew," Cupid said. "I think I'll leave you to it, Rudy. Have a fucking nice day."

And with that, he dropped about fifty feet in less than a second, turned a tight one-eighty, and pissed off in the other direction.

Rudolph smiled, then remembered where he was going and the smile fell from his face and landed on the back of a squirrel.

"Dropped your smile, mate!" the squirrel said, but Rudolph didn't hear it. "Deaf twat!" He didn't hear that either.

Arriving in, or over, Candycane Park, Rudolph's heart froze in his chest; he was really going to do this. Have a picnic with Merthyr. In broad daylight. When he was supposed to be sick. In the park. A picnic. With his stalker. In the park.

"This is a terrible idea," Rudolph told himself, but he was already scouring the scenery below, which looked a lot like this:

BABY RUDOLPH

Elf-mothers watched their elf-children as they went back and forth on the swings, round and round on the roundabout, up and down, up and down on the slide, in and out through the tunnel, under and over, under and over the climbing nets. Elf-mothers weren't really watching—they were smoking and talking about so-and-so from down the lane who had taken to sowing carnations in the middle of July, what an absolute idiot, they'll never come through, oh, and she's also having an affair with the milkman, but of course she is, that's why she's getting an extra gold-top on a Tuesday—but they were pretending to watch with such gusto that it was difficult to tell otherwise. So long as no one fell of the climbing frame, or got attacked by an XL bully, the kids'd be none the wiser. And while the elf-parents pretended to watch their crotch-goblins, other things were a-happening, too, such as the snow-ski fellas going round and round the park as if they owned the place. Speed was not a problem for these inconsiderate arseholes, and they made it all up as they went along. Leaping high over ramps they'd made from bits of wood and piles of bricks; the snow-ski fellas were a breed all of their own, and Rudolph wished that as a breed they would go extinct. Elderly elves sat opposite each other, playing chess and draughts, and in one case,

Operation! and as they played, they discussed all manner of important things, such as their latest test results from the doctor, how long they had left to live—"He's only given me another two-hundred years." "Oh, that's awful! I am sorry to hear that."—and what their wives were making for dinner. In the duck pond, fat ducks, all filled up on stale bread and chickpeas (whose fucking idea was that?) floated about the place, moaning and rubbing at their distended stomachs. Birds did bird things, squirrels did squirrel things, and a bunny did bird things, because it hadn't quite decided what it identified as yet. Overall, it was park scenery, seen all across the universe in every dimension, and it was enough to make Rudolph gag.

He was about to turn round and head back to his stable when he saw her, and he said, "Shit."

From above, she looked like a normal-sized reindeer—one without magic in its blood and therefore incapable of flight—had been dropped from a great height. From a space shuttle. And had gone splat! And from that shuttle, the elfstronauts all gazed down upon the Land of Christmas, to that particular park, and scratched their heads with confusion, because that massive blemish hadn't been there yesterday.

BABY RUDOLPH

Rudolph prepared everything for landing. Legs, check, nose glowing red, check, altitude check, check, and then a voice in his head said, *It's not too late, you know?*

"Oh, shut up!" Rudolph snapped. "Let's just get this over with."

The voice apologised and said no more.

There was already an almighty runway of displaced snow; Merthyr must have had a shitshow of a landing, and Rudolph wished he'd been there to see it. He was grateful that she'd cleared for him a path, though, and took advantage of it.

Fifty feet.

Forty.

Ten.

Legs down.

Flash nose.

And we are down, I repeat, we are down.

Rudolph slid the last twenty or so metres and came to a complete stop next to a picnic blanket, hamper, two wine glasses, and a big fat reindeer. Merthyr's face lit up when she saw him, and she stopped buttering crackers to give him her full, undivided attention.

"Rudy! You look wonderful!" she said, smiling. Then she stopped smiling, and she growled, "You're late, ya wee cretin." Then the smile returned. "Never mind, hey? Let's have a nice picnic."

Without speaking—he couldn't even if he tried—Rudolph took it all in. The wine glasses, the decanted Merlot, the tartan blanket, the condoms—

"They were here when I got here," she said, flicking the Durexes away with a massive hoof. "I hope you like food," she said, returning to her crackers.

"I know that *you* do," Rudolph said, under his breath.

"What was that, babeh Rudy?"

"I said of *course* I do," he said, in that panicked way people often do when they fear they've been caught out. He made a mental note not to mutter disparagingly again; she had awfully good hearing for a reindeer her size, whatever that meant.

Rudolph settled himself down on the snow beside the blanket; Merthyr looked at him as if he'd just offered her a gastric bypass.

"What's wrong?" she asked. "Don't like tartan, is that it? Are you prejudiced against blanket patterns that don't conform to your beliefs, Rudy? Are you a racist towards checks?"

Rudolph quickly bum-shuffled onto the blanket and giggled like a little girl. "No, of course not," he said. "I just didn't know how much space you needed, you know? How much food you'd brought, and therefore how much blanket you required for what must be a spread of epic proportions." He dry-swallowed. "Something like that."

Merthyr offered him a creepy smile; he politely declined it.

"You look nervous," she said, upending a packet of scratchings into a flowery, pink bowl. "Just relax, Rudy. I promise I won't gobble ye all up like a giant."

"Please don't," Rudolph whispered.

"What was that?"

"I said don't be silly," he said. "I've been looking forward to this all night, ever since you sent me that lovely invite."

"Ah, it's no bother," said she. "Wine?"

Rudolph nodded. "Yes, please. I love wine. The more the better, I say."

"Don't forget you have to fly me home later," she said, which fairly put the shits up him. "So, best not to be drinking too much, ma babeh Rudy. Otherwise you might not be able to get it up."

"Wh... what?" said Rudolph with eyes like saucers.

"My picnic basket," she said. "I mean, it won't be as heavy as it was on the way here, but it's still a good weight." She said 'good' as if it had about fifteen O's. "Shouldn't be a problem for a big, strapping magic reindeer like you, though, hey, Rudy?"

Rudolph wasn't often lost for words, but now he was. In fact, he was lost for languages, too. Nothing would come out... of the front end, at least.

Merthyr poured two large glasses of red, and then held hers up. "To us!" she said.

Rudolph accepted his glass, and just about managed to say, "To good friends," without choking on his own tongue.

Glasses were clinked, and glances were exchanged. Hers said, *The things I'm going to do to you... I hope you've got life insurance, ya wee bastard, because I'm gonna ride that face until you go blue.*

His said, *Please don't.*

The picnic itself was a decent affair. There were sandwiches of varying fillings—egg and cress, ham and cheese, cheese and cucumber, tuna and mayo, and cress and egg, which was just an egg and cress eaten upside-down—and crisps and nuts, and then there came the sweet stuff. Biscuits and cakes, drop scones and waffles. Rudolph was fairly sure that some or most of this food would kill an ordinary reindeer, but none of that seemed to matter. It tasted good, and he was tipsy from Merlot, so fuck it. When in Rome... although the Romans probably never saw such a magnificent spread, even those rich ones that liked to watch lions eat foreigners.

The best part of the picnic, however, was not the food. It was that the subject of his atrocious performance the previous night did not come up, not once, and that was miraculous, since that was pretty much all they had in common, really. He was there, and so was she, but whether she was protecting his feelings by not mentioning it, or if she had completely forgotten to humiliate him all over again by recounting the terrible event in minute detail, Rudolph didn't know. He was glad of its absence, though, and dare he say it, even grateful to Merthyr for choosing not to broach the subject.

"Come here," said Merthyr as she began to rummage through the picnic hamper.

"I couldn't eat another thing," Rudolph said, slurring a bit. He could see two of her now, which was awful.

"No, you saft sod," she said. "I want to take a selfie of us both."

"That's not how selfies work," said Rudolph, and it wasn't. "Plus, I don't like having my picture taken." Hiccup. "I never look good in them. It's my nose, you see. Glows up with the flash, like those human photos with the kids and the devil eyes and—"

"Stop your moaning and come here," Merthyr said, with feeling. She had a camera in her hoof now, and was already holding it at arm's length, ready to snap. Rudolph didn't think the camera would be far enough away to get them both in.

Perhaps we could ask the elfstronauts...

She grabbed his head and pulled him into shot. "This'll be a nice way of remembering our first picnic, babeh Rudy," she said, and her breath smelt all onion-y and cheese-y and tuna-y, and a good combination it did not make. "Say troosers," she added.

"What?"

"Troosers, ya silly cunt! Say troosers. Say troosers, ya prick!"

BABY RUDOLPH

"Troosers!" Rudolph said, which seemed to make her smile.

The camera flashed and Merthyr released Rudolph from what was essentially a headlock, the kind that was not only illegal in certain sports but was also frowned upon in most dimensions. It was the kind of headlock that required a safe word. And Rudolph was glad to be free of it.

"Right, we've had a lovely time, haven't we?" said Rudolph, clapping his hooves together, "and there is now a photograph to prove it, which is nice, so I should be—"

"Oh, no," said Merthyr. "I know you're not just going to fly off and leave me, babeh Rudy. Oh, no, no, no," and she clicked her tongue violently. "That simply won't do. I have a whole afternoon planned, ma babeh. Tickets to the indoor skating disco. A two-hour slot at the fucking zoo, Rudy. Clay penguin shooting, ma babeh, all booked up, so you can't go, ya wee fucker, we're not even halfway done. Ma dates are in the history books, ya wee pelican, so you ain't goin' nowhere until I say so, do you hear me, ya wee bucket of fanny batter?"

Temperatures are known to drop suddenly and severely in the Land of Christmas, but quite often that is down to Mother Nature just doing her thing, as she is wont to do, and no one mentions it because it's completely normal behaviour for the weather.

Rudolph was an icicle. A magic reindeer-shaped icicle sitting on a tartan blanket in the middle of a park. His jaw had, at some point, dropped wide open and had frozen there. A fly popped into his mouth, had a good look around as if considering buying the place, did a quick shit behind one of the molars, and left. You wouldn't have had time to count the fingers on a twice-convicted Saudi shoplifter before Rudolph had turned into statuary.

"Gnn," he said, which was strange, because he could have sworn he'd meant to say, *Please, let me go home.*

"No need to thank me, babeh Rudy," she went on, and why not? He was in no fit state to respond. "Let's get all of this mess packed up, yeah? Then we can get over to the indoor skating disco, give me plenty of time to stuff my blisters into a pair of boots two sizes too small."

Rudolph managed a nod; every inch of his body was suddenly in pain.

"Well, come on, Rudy," she said, clicking her hoof in front of his motionless face. "Lots to do, ma wee buddy with benefits."

BABY RUDOLPH

Rudolph wished one of the benefits was that he could instantly disappear.

13

Once Jimbo had calmed down and returned to his natural colour, he seemed to be more open to the opportunity he now had, thanks to Finklefoot and The Fat Bastard.

"So, you asked him to let me help?" he said as he and Finklefoot walked down the High Street.

Finklefoot shoved a doughnut into his face and chewed for about thirty seconds before he was able to answer. "I told him I needed someone smart, someone with balls, someone I'd trust with my firstborn child."

All lies of course, but pleasant little, white ones, like, *No, I haven't seen your copy of the Lingerie Catalogue 2024*, and, *Cucumbers? I didn't know we had any cucumbers.*

"And he suggested me?" Jimbo asked, skilfully dodging a pram-pushing shopper. "I find it hard to believe that, out of all the elves at his disposal, we're the best he's got to oversee this."

"Me, too," Finklefoot said, and he meant it. "But there you have it. Like a shadow cabinet, like it or lump it we've got the job." He turned another doughnut over in his little hand, looked through the hole in it at Jimbo. "Is there a monocle shop around here? I really think, if we're taking this seriously, I should have some sort of gimmick."

"What? Like Poirot's moustache?"

"And Ironside's wheelchair," Finklefoot said.

"You'd have to get shot and paralysed by a sniper," Jimbo said, "otherwise people will say it's bad form. You can't pretend to be in a wheelchair if there's nothing wrong with you. It really pisses those cabbages off."

"I think calling them cabbages," said Finklefoot, "is also a faux pas."

"So, what's *my* gimmick?" Jimbo asked, changing the subject as quickly as possible before the cabbages cottoned on. "What would *my* thing be, if we're having one?"

Finklefoot thought about it hard. "Well, Kojak has his lollipops and his catchphrase, and Columbo has his raincoat and his, "Just one more thing" thing. Then there's Jane Marple, and she's just a batty old tart, and Jessica Fletcher, who should really stay away from glamorous events, because that's when someone always gets killed, she's a mystery writer solving mysteries. Barnaby Miller drinks a lot of milk, and Shawn Spencer has the fake psychic routine. Jim Rockford had his car, and Sherlock was just a cocky cunt, made famous by the catchphrase, No shit, Sherlock!"

"I'm pretty sure no one ever said that before or during Holmes' greatest adventures," Jimbo said, kicking a crawling toddler into the road.

"Of course they did, man!" said Finklefoot, and left it at that, for he hadn't an example to hand.

"So, what's my gimmick, then?" Jimbo asked again. "If you're having the monocle—"

"You could always have the *other* monocle," Finklefoot said. "They invariably come as a pair, usually connected in the middle, and you have to snap them in half, probably."

Jimbo shook his head. What he knew about monocles you could count on the fingers of his children's hands. The answer was nothing, because he was unfortunately seedless, and had been since falling out of a tree as a child.

"Pince-nez!" Finklefoot suddenly blurted.

"Prince who?" Jimbo replied, looking about the place and expecting to see royalty.

"That can be your thing," Finklefoot said, seemingly pleased with his own brilliance. "Pince-nez."

"Eff-eff, I have no idea what that means." He liked calling Finklefoot 'Eff-eff'. *That* could be his thing. Like Dr. Watson used to always say to Sherlock, *Will you stop showing off, prick. Some of us have real jobs.*

"Here we are," said Finklefoot, dragging Jimbo by the arm into a store and marching straight up to the counter, where sat a small elf with a big nose and the biggest pair of bifocals Jimbo had ever seen in his life. Veritable bottle-bases, these glasses, and they made the elf's eyes huge, as if he were on some sort of class-A substance.

"How may I help you gentlemen?" said the elf, whose name-badge said **TREVOR - HE/HIM - "I LOVE MY JOB!"**

"Good morning, Trevor!" said Finklefoot. He was starting to enjoy himself, and the best way to get through this whole thing, he had realised, was to really embrace the role, and get Method, if he had to, like De Niro in *Taxi Driver*, or De Niro in *Raging Bull*, or De Niro in—

"What *do* we want?" Jimbo asked, giving Finklefoot a little shin-kick.

"Ah, yes!" said Finklefoot. "We would like to purchase one-and-a-half pairs of glasses."

Trevor looked at them both as if they had just threatened him with a good time. His face said, *You taking the piss?* while his body said, *I haven't seen a doctor in over a hundred years.*

"Allow me to elaborate," said Finklefoot.

"Please do," Trevor said with about as much enthusiasm as one of those hara-kiri fellas.

"I'm looking for one monocle, and one pair of pince-nez."

"You've come to the right place," said Trevor, gesturing to the millions of pairs of eye-correctors all around and about the place. His sarcasm was duly noted, and Finklefoot made a mental note not to tip the speccy bastard.

"I still don't know what a pince-nez is," said Jimbo.

"It means pinch nose," Finklefoot said. "I believe it's German, and was a term often used when, during the second world war, the soldiers grew bored of waiting in their trenches for anything exciting to happen, so they invented a game called Pinch Nose, and in the game you had to pinch the nose of your fellow soldier when they weren't looking, and as you did you had to call out, as loudly as you could so that the dratted English might hear and decide to engage, 'Pinch Nose!', and if you managed to start a battle with the enemy, you won the game and had first dibs on the jewellery stripped from the dead bodies of the Ally forces."

Jimbo was speechless.

Trevor was not.

"It's French," he said. "The only bit out of all that bullshit was that it means 'pinch nose'."

"Yes, well, shuffle on and grab a pair, will you?" Finklefoot said with a face you could toast marshmallows by. Jimbo hadn't seen anything that red since his dog's dick had come out at a furry convention.

Trevor went away and disappeared through a door behind the counter.

"That was a lovely story," Jimbo said, stifling laughter. "German soldiers, indeed..."

Finklefoot didn't dignify this with a response; instead, he stared at his own face in one of those vertical mirror things they have wherever reading or sunglasses are sold.

Starting to look old, me old chum, me old pal, he thought.

Jimbo was trying on sunglasses—about the most superfluous purchase in the Land of Christmas, apart from skinny jeans and a TV license—when Trevor returned with two boxes.

"Ah!" said Finklefoot. "Our gimmicks have arrived!"

Trevor took the lids off the boxes. "Which one of you wants the German battle-starters and which one is the Cyclops?"

Having paid for their respective gimmicks, Finklefoot and Jimbo left the store somewhat rejuvenated. A second wind, some might call it, but not Finklefoot or Jimbo, to whom a second wind meant after-supper flatulence.

"You didn't have to smash his glass bottles," Jimbo said, trying to get his pince-nez to stay put on the bridge of his hooter.

"He should have seen it coming," said Finklefoot, pushing the monocle into place and trying not to get all tangled up in the dangly bit. "Especially with those lenses."

"Right!" said Jimbo, almost tripping over a homeless elf, for he couldn't see much, and what he could see was twice the size it should be. "Where to, Sherlock?"

"Elephantry, my dear Jimbo," said Finklefoot. "Off to Ahora's house we go."

*

In the dim living-room, a cat, sensing something amiss, suddenly straightened up and growled at the door. Starving, this cat was, for it had eaten everything its owner had put out for it three days prior, and had since gone round looking for insects and crumbs, but after a few hours had come to the conclusion that there was nothing edible, and it was best just to curl up on the back of its owner's armchair and die without further ado. It was taking a bloody long time, though, and so the cat, Buttercup, had considered suicide, but after two hours of trying to get the caps off child-safety bottles in the bathroom, and a further hour trying to make a noose from its owner's unfinished knitting project, it had arrived at the unfortunate conclusion that it would just have to die of natural causes.

Such is life.

Then, when all seemed lost, Buttercup heard voices coming from the kitchen, and more accurately, the back door which opened onto the kitchen.

"Right!" said one of the voices. "Pick the lock, if you would."

"I don't know how to pick a lock," said a second, slightly deeper voice. It was the kind of voice that wore pince-nez, the cat thought. "I thought it'd be open."

"Well, it's not open, is it?" said the first voice again. Buttercup felt it belonged to the person in charge, the head honcho, he who shall be listened to and then probably ignored.

The cat, she leapt gracefully down from the back of her owner's armchair, and slowly moved toward the kitchen. Neither of the voices belonged to her owner, which confirmed the cat's suspicions that she would turn up dead at some point during the plot, and it was now every cat for itself. Confirmation had never tasted so bitter.

"Just fucking kick it in!" said the first voice.

"That's breaking and entering," replied the second. "You can get exiled for that."

"Not us," said the first. "The Fat Bastard's on our side. He told me to do whatever it takes to find out where Ahora is, bring her abductor-slash-killer to justice, and, failing all that, find the spare key to the jigsaw factory so that those lazy bastards can all get back to work, so put your foot through this door right now and become the hero you've always dreamed of being."

"I've always dreamed of owning one of those little cubicles in the middle of big malls that sells mobile-phone cases and vape-pens and fixes broken laptop screens," said the second voice.

"Yeah, that *is* a cushy little number," said the first voice. "Never seem busy, do they?"

"My kind of job, that."

BABY RUDOLPH

There came a sudden rattle and a click, and the cat did one final shit before darting out through the back door, through the legs of both elves, and went off to find something to eat that wasn't dust or its own faeces.

"Oh, it *was* open," said Finklefoot. "Fancy that!"

They entered Ahora's back door (it's okay, they had consent) and found themselves standing in a rather splendid kitchen. Everything was exceedingly neat and tidy, with a place for everything and everything in its place. But there wasn't half a stink of piss.

"Cat, I reckon," said Jimbo, for he, too, was taking his newly-appointed role as detective seriously. "Stings the eyes, doesn't it."

"Just the one," said Finklefoot, blinking tears away from the un-monocled eye, "Right," he went on, "let's give this place a thorough going over. You start upstairs, I'll start down here, and we'll meet in the middle."

Jimbo frowned. "But then we'll just both be stood in the middle of the stairs," he said, for he was a lot smarter than he looked.

"You're right," said Finklefoot. "Scratch that. Just meet back here in five. *Goddamit* that kitty-litter's worse than peeling onions with your own eyelids!"

"Suck a spoon," Jimbo said as he headed toward the stairs.

"How dare you!" Finklefoot called after him. "Right, let's have a look..."

The kitchen was clearly a bust; there was nothing lying about, nothing broken to suggest a scuffle, no blood spatters up the wall to signify someone got all slashed up like a Halloween pumpkin, nothing, nothing, nothing. The only criminal activity was the cat-litter tray underneath the sink. Finklefoot didn't know whether to put it outside or take it down to the station for Quim and Dufflecoat to deal with.

Finklefoot was glad to move on to the next room—the living-room, or if your parents had money and you weren't allowed to wear your shoes in the house, the *lounge*—where the ammonia had been diluted with clean air to create something in-between that was still unpleasant, but not enough to make you want to tear your eyes out or pull a plastic bag down over your head, tie a ribbon round it, and pop yourself outside next to the other trash.

The living-room-cum-lounge was tidy, but there were signs that life had once existed here: the empty teacup sitting on a small table next to the armchair; the magazine lying open on an article about one woman's distress at discovering her husband was also her father and sister; the unfinished knitting on the armchair, which was what appeared to be the beginnings of a tea cosy, but someone or something had tried to fashion it into a noose, for some reason.

"Nah," Finklefoot said. "It's just the way the wool fell, that's all." Which is why most feline depression goes unnoticed until it's far too late.

Signs of life, there might have been, but nothing to suggest the crime—if indeed there had been one at all; Finklefoot was starting to grow a little sceptical about the whole thing—had taken place here in Ahora's home.

Just then, there were thumps on the staircase, and a moment later Jimbo came into the room. "Nothing upstairs," he said. "But you should see the bottom drawer in her bedroom. She don't half like Daleks."

"I fear," said Finklefoot, "that we are looking in the wrong place. If there was a struggle, it didn't happen here, and if it did this elfnapper of ours has done a magnificent job of cleaning up."

Jimbo shrank a little, or appeared to. It's hard to shrink even more when you're already an elf. I mean, how low can you go?

"My dear friend," said Finklefoot. "Let us depart this den of sterility where, apart from that litter tray, everything is just so. Our investigation moves on!" And with that he did a half-twirl, pinched his nose between thumb and forefinger, and marched toward the open back door and the fresh air beyond.

Not to be outdone, Jimbo did the same, only with more finesse. Once outside, the world came back into focus, and both Finklefoot and Jimbo doubled over and sucked in huge lungfuls of air.

"You don't realise what it's doing to you, really," said Jimbo. "No wonder so many old people die in their sleep. It's not from age; it's cat-piss."

Jimbo was drooling and spitting and going, *Geeehhhhrrr.* "I don't think," he said, removing his pince-nez and wiping the lenses with his shirt cuff, "these helped much. For something called Pinch Nose, they're not particularly good at it. It's like calling me Great in Bed."

Finklefoot threw up into the snow; he'd been doing so well, too, but that had pushed him over the edge. "I don't think the smell is ever going to leave," he said. "And my vision is compromised, even with the monocle."

"We'll be okay," Jimbo said, straightening up. "I think the worst of it is over." He paused, stuck his tongue out, and said,

"Yeah, I can taste the snow again. I think we're going to be okay."

"Thank fuck for that," said Finklefoot. "Trixie's doing beef bourguignon tonight and it's bad enough without an underlying hint of two-day-old cat-piss."

Jimbo put on his pince-nez—he felt smarter with them on, even if he did look like a pillock—and began to make his way back to the gate. Finklefoot followed, still spitting and hacking.

Telepathically, between them, a conclusion had been reached, and that was this:

Pub?

Yes, pub.

And it was on the way to The Partridge Inn that they arrived at a certain alleyway with the intention of passing through it and thusly undercutting their current destination arrival time by about three minutes. Finklefoot led the way, but only because Jimbo's right shoe had come off in the snow about five minutes prior and, having found it and put it back on, was still trying to catch up to his Sherlock.

"What's that, Eff-eff?" said Jimbo suddenly, and he did pointings in the general direction of the thing at which he was pointing.

Finklefoot looked at the finger and said, "I'd say it was a bogey, Jimbo. What have I told you about picking—"

"Not the finger," Jimbo said, taking an am-dram step forward. "There's a patch where the snow won't stick. Up there. Can you see it? I wonder if it means something. Even more crazy and completely by chance, what if it has something to do with our case?" He began to turn his head and gazed into the space where a camera would have fit quite nicely.

"Shut up," Finklefoot said. "There will be no breaking the fourth wall on my watch. You're not Phoebe Waller-Bridge and this isn't *Fleabag.*" He was, however, intrigued as he got closer to the patch of alleyway where the snow wouldn't stick. It was, of course, the exact spot Hattie Quim had taken a lengthy piss the previous night, and her urine—there's a lot of that in this chapter, but be assured, it's all coincidence, and by this time the otherworldly biographer is as much in the dark as you are—had stretched out and out and, much like when the juice goes on your slushy, down and down, creating a six-by-four patch of clear concrete. Marvellous, it was, and Finklefoot's mouth fell open, for he hadn't seen the ground in years. Not since someone set fire to his wheelie-bin.

BABY RUDOLPH

Reaching the magnificent anomaly (or piss-patch, if you will) Finklefoot's monocled eye fell upon something white, fluttering gently in the wind and yet stuck to the ground, either by something adhesive or by sheer willpower.

"Just a hanky," Jimbo said, for he was still reading his colleague's mind from the pub telepathy whatchamacallit.

Finklefoot dropped into a crouch—which is always funny to see if you get the chance and you know a little person who doesn't mind—and peeled the hanky from the concrete.

"This chapter's getting sicker by the second," said Jimbo, who was still standing and looking terribly affected by everything going on around him without his say so.

Finklefoot examined the handkerchief and found it to be clean. No snot or bogies at all. And no blood, either, which was splendid. He gave it a quick sniff, and that was all it took. He almost toppled over backwards from whatever was on the offending article, but he knew what it was. He'd had dalliances with it before.

"Chloroform," said Finklefoot.

"It's a bit early for paperwork," said Jimbo, because that's how terrible jokes work.

Finklefoot held up the handkerchief and got to his feet, rather unsteadily. "This handkerchief has been, at some point relevant to our timeline, whatever that is now, soaked in chloroform."

"Why would someone soak a hanky in chloroform?" Jimbo said. And also, "And what's chloroform?"

Finklefoot produced a transparent plastic bag from his coat pocket, emptied his sandwiches out of it, and put the hanky in. It wasn't exactly CSI-approved, but Finklefoot was working with what he had.

"There is only one reason for soaking a hanky in chloroform," he said. "And that is for the purposes of putting someone into the Land of Nod so that you might extract their body from the point of attack to the place of current whereabouts."

Jimbo shook his head; this was all getting a bit convoluted, for his liking.

"Ahora, our victim who is yet to show up dead, was taken from this very spot." Finklefoot turned and examined the ground again. "And what is that I see?" he said, for he couldn't see it at all, really, not from where he was standing, and not with a monocle whose prescription could have been for anyone. But he made out a shape with his one good eye, and took two steps until he was hovering, still dizzy from the hanky, over it.

"Is that a—"

"I believe so," said Finklefoot.

"But why would—"

"Don't give anything away just yet," said Finklefoot, tapping the side of his nose. "There's still quite a bit to get through."

He bagged up the secret item and smiled. "This could lead us straight to the elfnapper," he said. "And to Ahora, so that we may rescue her and become heroes once again."

Jimbo, who had never been a hero before in his life, said, "But what if it's just an ordinary—"

"Da!" said Finklefoot. "You'll ruin the ending, you wally."

14

"Oh, look! Another fucking seal!"

Merthyr was clearly having a whale of a time at the zoo, but there were, Rudolph thought, only so many times you could hear a woman celebrate the appearance of a penguin before your primal urges took over and you just pushed them into the polar bear enclosure. He was grumpy already, after the clusterfuck that had been the indoor skating disco, at which Merthyr had taken it upon herself to clear the ice and channel both Torvill *and* fucking Dean in what can only be described as the most embarrassing thing ever to happen on ice since the captain of the Titanic stated the bloody obvious. Elves and other beings had laughed and pointed as Merthyr threw herself about the place as if she had just dropped out of her mother, landed directly on her head, and decided she wanted to be a figure skater when she was older, and to hell with cranial fractures and subsequent brain herniation. *This girl's gonna skate! Gonna skate good, this girl! Derrrr.*

And now they were at the zoo, and Merthyr was full of beans—and sandwiches, and cakes, and pies, and…—and dragging Rudolph from one place to the other by the reluctant hoof. *The vivarium, the aquarium, the fucking butterfly house with the pretty little wings and the... with the landing on you, and the... fucking moths!* Rudolph had thought, angrily. *I'm in a room hot enough to fry eggs and I'm covered in fucking moths, and she's loving it! Look at her, all bouncy and laughing, like some influencer twat who's just discovered how maps work.*

"Oh, isn't this wonderful, babeh Rudy!" she joyfully exclaimed as they left the butterfly house. Rudolph was just glad to be back on the outside, where it was cold, snowy, and familiar. His back was sore from carrying the picnic hamper, and he really needed a lie down somewhere quiet, somewhere cool, and somewhere that didn't charge thirty-eight zoo-dollars for the privilege.

"You know what we should see next?" Merthyr said, unfolding the giant map and scanning it with all the enthusiasm of a newly-appointed ecclesiastic being introduced to a roomful of altar-boys. "They've got reindeer! Rudy, they've got some plain old, non-magical reindeer!"

It was hard to get excited about magicless reindeer, and Merthyr asking him to do so was like telling him to transmogrify himself into a spider.

It couldn't be done.

"I really should be getting home," said Rudolph, quietly, as if not to startle Merthyr.

Whether she heard him or not made no difference, because Merthyr was so captivated by the zoo map—fifteen zoo-dollars, and with a coupon for 10% off their next visit—that she completely ignored him, and said: "And then after we've seen the reindeer, there's a Wild West-themed food court right next to it. We can get something to eat before we see the flamingos."

Her strange accent, Rudolph noticed, had all but disappeared; further proof that she was as mad as a box of frogs. Who in their right mind simply reserved one accent for happy times, and another for psychotic breakdowns? That wasn't just nuts, it was terrifying.

And here I am at the zoo with it, holding hooves and pretending it's okay, normal, nothing to see here but two magical reindeer, one average-sized, the other looking like it ate average-sized for breakfast, and she's wearing a pink cardigan and a perm that'd give 80s Dolly Parton a run for her money.

"I said," Rudolph said, hoping that she might respond this time, "that I have a lot to be getting on with, and—"

BABY RUDOLPH

"Getting on with?" Merthyr spun around so quickly, so angrily, that the three moths and two butterflies that had hidden in her perm to break out of the butterfly house once and for all, were immediately displaced. "What have ye to be gettin' on with, ya wee broken biscuit?" She dropped the map and brought her front legs down on it, hooves squashing it into the snow. "I'd like to know, Rudy, what a lazy, unfunny, ungrateful, uninterested, uncanny-looking little red-nosed cunt like you has to be getting on with."

All around, elves were staring in their direction. One elf-child in particular was invested. "Is she going to beat him up?" the child asked its father, who was also intrigued. It was the popcorn that gave it away. "I don't know, son," he told the child. "But I don't fancy his chances." The elf-child began to clap. "Yay!" it said. And also, "Give him one for me, sister!"

There is a myth, well-known if you're into that sort of thing, that reindeer do not know how to blush, that it's simply not in their genes, and that even if they could, would anyone really care?

Well Rudolph was putting that myth to bed quicker than naughty children. His face had turned the colour of beets; even his antlers were blushing.

"That's what I thought, babeh Rudy," said Merthyr, picking the giant map back up and knocking the snow and sludge from it. "Honestly," she went on, "I'm your girlfriend, Rudy, not your wee sugar-deer. We'll be having no more nonsense about being somewhere else, babeh Rudy, is that clear?"

Rudolph managed to get the hinge in his neck to work, just about, and he nodded with all the enthusiasm of an ecclesiastic being arrested for, pending further investigation, fingering twenty-seven minors in the back of a Sunday School bus. (see previous ecclesiastic simile for further details, but we should have all seen it coming).

"Right!" said Merthyr, chirpily. "Let's go see what a non-magical reindeer looks like." She reached for Rudolph's foreleg and, once she had it, pulled him up into bipedal mode.

Like most human people, Rudolph hated walking around on two legs. Unnatural, it was, and apart from the fact that it just looked plain silly, you really felt it the next day.

Not only was Rudolph unhappy about having to walk round the zoo with a raving lunatic, but he was also now having to do it with one front leg behind his back, holding on for dear life to Merthyr's picnic hamper.

The magicless reindeer, it transpired, looked just like them. Apart from the red nose and precariously balanced wicker hamper, and the ability to walk for long periods of time on two legs, and, in Merthyr's case, the ability to not only know of a hairdresser, but also to book in bi-monthly to have her hair fucked up, but apart from that they looked just like them.

Rudolph wanted to go home.

To lock the stable door.

And to cry.

No chapter should finish on such a morose image, and so when one of the magicless reindeer kicked a turd that bounced off that impudent little elf-child's head, it came as something of a relief.

*

"I need," said Rudolph to the Sherlockian policeman behind the reception desk, "to report a stalker." Relief flooded his system like a hole in the Channel Tunnel. The idea that he was safe now, free of Merthyr, that dreadful, hideous bully of a cow, was almost too much for Rudolph to take all at once, and his legs seemingly turned to jelly. It was only the desk keeping him up.

The police officer looked at Rudolph, and continued looking until he figured it out. Eventually, and rather pleased with himself, he said, "Rudolph! The red-nosed reindeer!" And then he started singing the song and doing a little dance to go with it; Rudolph checked the corners of the room for cameras, because if this was one of those shows with the pranks, he was going to be royally pissed off. "Jeez, Rudolph the red-nosed reindeer," said the officer, pulling his trousers back up and fastening his shirt buttons. Rudolph had had no idea what that part of the dance was all about, and was already in the process of deleting it from the Recent Memories section of his brain.

The officer took his seat and cleared his throat. "So, what can I do for you, Rudolph?" he said, but before Rudolph could repeat the crimes against him, the officer said, "Don't tell me! Caught speeding, come for forgiveness? Sleigh parked in a disabled bay, The Fat Bastard's sent you to dispute it? No? New regulations on glowing noses, yours is too bright, come to get it dimmed in the name of public safety?"

BABY RUDOLPH

I'll dim your fucking nose in a minute, Rudolph thought. "I've already told you once," he said, trying to remain calm. "I'm being stalked and I'm here to report it."

"Stalked, you say?" said a besuited man as he emerged from a room to the right of the desk and closed the door behind him. "What's that, like some sort of euphemism? Like, I met this fella who's into forest foreplay, and now I'm getting stalked—"

"It means," said Rudolph, wondering just what was in the water in these parts, "that someone is harassing me, and I'm not only scared for my life, I'm also concerned for the lives of everyone who has ever seen snow."

"Hm," said the suited elf as he took to his desk and produced a notepad and pen from somewhere. "My name's Chief Quim, this is Officer Dufflecoat."

Rudolph nodded at them both, which was as far as the pleasantries went.

"Now, explain to me," said Chief Quim, "clearly, and without use of big words, just what the hell is going on." He ate a Tic-Tac, smoked a cigarette, and ate a turkey-mustard sandwich, which was surely the wrong order in which to do those things, but there you go. Rudolph, who had been trying to figure out the best way to start, finally spoke.

"She's a bloody nutter!" he said. "I mean, you wouldn't let this one look after your kids if you wanted to ever see them again. Grade A fucking nightmare! In fact, she makes Bela Lugosi sleep with a night-light. Frightens the shit out of me, she does, and I'm terrified that one of these days, she's gonna smash my stable door in and say, 'Here's Merthyr!', and I just don't know who to turn to. I used to be brave, but since I met this freak yesterday, I've become pussified."

Chief Quim took it all down while Officer Dufflecoat gnawed at the stem of his Calabash pipe.

"And you say this freak, this nightmare, this veritable serial-killer of a woman is called Merthyr?" he said, boring holes into Rudolph's face with his eyes. *Those are not the eyes of a smart man,* Rudolph thought. *They are the eyes of a man who delegates to a smart man and then takes all the credit for it.* So perhaps not as dumb as he looked.

"That's right," Rudolph said. "Merthyr Titful. But she's not a woman, she's a reindeer, a magical one, like me—"

"Oooh," said Chief Quim. "Someone likes to blow his own trumpet."

"I wish *I* could," said Officer Dufflecoat, before quickly adding, "Not his! *Mine.* I wish I could... blow—"

BABY RUDOLPH

"Anyway," said Chief Quim, much to everyone's delight. "So, this Merthyr, the magical reindeer, she's been harassing you, making your life a living nightmare? Well, that sounds terrible, and we can't be having that, so please, in your own time and in your own words, because no one else's will make much sense, tell me what she has done in all the grisly details." Without looking up from his notepad, he jabbed the pen in Rudolph's direction, the universal gesture for: *And, go!*

Rudolph thought for a moment, and quickly realised he was in trouble. Made much worse when he started talking. "Well, it all started yesterday at training. I was writing on my lunch-break and—"

"Writing?" Chief Quim said. "But you're a reindeer, lacking the necessary dexterity in which to even hold a pen, let alone create meaningful sentences with it."

"That's what makes us magical," Rudolph said, if for nothing else but posterity. "Can I continue?"

"I don't know," Quim said, shaking his head. "Can you?"

Like a blindfolded fencer, this caught him off-guard.

"I think so, yes," he said.

"Then please," said the Chief, returning to his notepad. "But try to make it more exciting. Both me and my pen are running out of patience."

"Okay, so I was writing some new jokes in the stable—"

"You were writing jokes?" It was Officer Dufflecoat's turn to interrupt, apparently. "As in, funny-funny, ha-ha, tell me another one, skipper, 'cos I've just pissed me knickers, that sort of thing?"

"I see you are familiar with the concept," said Rudolph, sarcastically.

Officer Dufflecoat frowned and his deerstalker went to the left. "But you're a flying reindeer with a fog-resistant schnozz," he said. "Why were you writing jokes?"

"I'm a stand-up comic as well," Rudolph said, fearing that he would be here all day. "I've got a slot in the Land of Christmas Annual Variety Show—"

"Ah, yes!" said Chief Quim. "That veritable feast of entertainment that comes but once a year, and then fucks off for the rest of it. A bit like The Fat Bastard, some might say, and if they do, I have been instructed to arrest them." He sighed, then went on, "Of course, I won't be performing this year, but my wife, my beautiful Hattie, Mrs Quim, she's taken charge of the choir. Although they're not nailed on to win, I've recently placed a bet with my local bookmaker at odds of no less than sixty-to-one. Gosh, can you believe that?

BABY RUDOLPH

Easy money, anyway, come on you little magical comedian twat, none of us is getting any younger."

Rudolph tried to recall where he had got up to in his story. Ah, yes! Cornered in the stable. "Anyway, there I was, just minding my business when she came in. Merthyr Titful—"

"How are you spelling that?" asked Officer Dufflecoat.

"Why does that matter to you?" replied Rudolph. "He's the one with the pen." He nodded in Chief Quim's direction.

"I know how to spell it," said the Chief. "This isn't the first time her name has crossed my desk."

Somewhere off in the distance, a choir of angels began to sing. One of them was slightly off-key, though, and it ruined the whole thing.

"She's done this before?" asked Rudolph, and of course it made perfect sense. You didn't get as scary as she was now overnight; no, it took practice, probably *years* of it. There were likely hundreds of victims lying, trampled and sex-exhausted, in her wake, and he was just another notch on the psychopathic cow's antler...

"Nah," said Chief Quim with a grin. "But the look on your face was priceless."

"Oh," said Rudolph. "Shall I continue with my report, or would you like me to turn around and bend over so that you can shaft me good and proper?"

"Please," said the Chief, "do go on."

"I stood up for her, you see," Rudolph said as the whole thing played in his head like an 8mm horror movie, with music by Christopher Young and special effects by Tom Savini. "She's a big girl, you see, this Merthyr. Some might say morbidly obese," he went on, "but me? I'd say she could do with a dietician, yes, of course, and perhaps a consistent exercise regime, sure, but morbidly obese?" Slight pause. How could he say this without upsetting or triggering anyone? "I'd say that she's built like two brick shithouses, concreted together and then covered over with jelly and meat."

"Very diplomatic," Dufflecoat said, approvingly. "You'd make a great politician."

"Well, the others," Rudolph continued, "they came into the stable, and they were bullying her, and I stood up for her." He hadn't expected a medal, but a simple salute would have sufficed. When it didn't come, Rudolph shrugged and said, "My life's been a living hell since. And Merthyr is the demon at the bottom of the pit."

BABY RUDOLPH

Chief Quim stopped writing. In fact, he had stopped writing at first mention of 'morbidly obese' and had taken to doodling fatties ever since.

"I can see that you are upset," said the Chief. "Would you like for me to pass you a box of tissues?"

"Do you have one?"

"No. Now, I'd like to hear how Ms. Titful has ruined your life in the space of," he checked his watch, "eighteen hours."

So Rudolph let them have it. The whole shebang, including but not limited to: how she had appeared at his Secret Comedy Club gig and saved his ass when the audience turned on him; how she had taken hundreds of pictures of him without his knowledge and then posted them to MyFace; how she had messaged him with an invite to a picnic; how said picnic had turned into an afternoon of absolute nightmarish episodes stitched together with grazing interludes; firstly an indoor skating disco; second, the awful zoo trip, and then the afternoon concluding with clay penguin shooting, at which he was terrible, but not so Merthyr, who had all the accuracy of Chris Kyle and had taken apart so many clay penguins that Rudolph didn't know whether to cheer or call the RSPCA.

"The only reason I'm even here now," said Rudolph, breathing hard, "is because I told her I was meeting up with some of my training buddies to discuss climate change and the effect it's having on our exposed undercarriages whilst in flight mode."

Chief Quim looked across to Officer Dufflecoat, who in turn looked up at Rudolph, whose gaze fell upon Quim. It was like the ending of Reservoir Dogs, but without all the gun-pointing and bad language.

Eventually, the Chief held aloft his notepad and tapped his pen against it. "What does that look like to you?"

Rudolph looked. "It looks like a picture of lots of fat people," he said. "And one of them has a speech bubble that says, Oh no! How did we ever get this way?'"

"It's a mystery, ain't it?" said Chief Quim, dropping his notepad down onto the desk. "Anyway, back to your predicament."

"Not much of a predicament, Chief," Officer Dufflecoat said, sucking on his Calabash. He struck Rudolph as the kind of elf that would hold a lift door for you, but just until you got within reach, and then allow it to shut. Prick.

Chief Quim nodded and said, "Hm." If Dufflecoat was the sonofabitch that would close a lift door on you, Quim

BABY RUDOLPH

was the guy already in the lift, watching it all unfold and laughing, "What you are telling me," he said, "and correct me if I'm wrong, though that very rarely happens, but this Merthyr, who you claim is a fiend from the bowels of Hell, yes, your words, not mine. This Merthyr, she supported you last night at a gig in which you were bombing, then shared some delightful pictures from the event in what can only be described as a show of unwavering support, and then invited you to a splendid picnic in the park, at which you partook in sundry pastries, sarnies, and exotic fruits, before accompanying you on an all-expenses paid trip about the tourist attractions—the disco, the zoo, the clay penguin shooting—and instead of thanking this woman—"

"Big fat Reindeer—"

"Instead of *thanking* this reindeer for such a wonderful time, you want to have her arrested?" Chief Quim's frown was so deep, you could have buried a whole deck of cards in there.

"No... you've put it a *nice* way... I..." Rudolph was, like a dictionary dipped in white paint, lost for words. When put the way the Chief had just put it, of *course* it sounded silly. Ridiculous and selfish, but perhaps it was because he hadn't told it right.

"I'm afraid that no crime has been committed," said the besuited elf as he clicked and clacked his pen in that infuriating way bank managers do when they realise you've exhausted your overdraft, sold the house and one of the kids, and will still be defaulting on this month's building and contents insurance.

"But she's dangerous!" whined Rudolph.

"Yes. A worthy successor to Jack the Ripper," Chief Quim laughed. "Lock up your husbands and sons, there is a beast on the streets who will torture you relentlessly with free scones and walkthrough tours of Grade II listed buildings."

"Stay out of the shadows," said Officer Dufflecoat theatrically. "She'll feed you up until you're fit to burst, and then take you on a nice half-board holiday to the Cotswolds!"

"Check your children's closets before you go to bed, because she might be in there, Merthyr the Merciless, icing cookies and sorting out environmentally-friendly field-trips to the countryside where she'll teach your kids all about how to make grenades out of pine-cones and explosive tripwires out of vines and a triple-A battery."

"All right, cunts!" shouted Rudolph, which had the desired effect. The Chief and the Officer settled back down in their seats. "I get that it doesn't sound like she's done anything—"

"Because she hasn't—"

"—but I'm telling you, Merthyr is dangerous, and I'm scared of her, and you should be, too."

"Why?" asked Officer Dufflecoat. "She's not stalking us."

Rudolph sighed, took several deep breaths before continuing. "Can you at least keep an eye on her? I'm pretty sure she knows where I live, and I can guarantee if I was to buy a bunny today, it would end up boiling in a pot by this time tomorrow."

"Then why buy the bunny in the first place?" Dufflecoat said.

"If you buy the bunny," said Chief Quim, "I might have to arrest you for premeditated murder—"

"I'm not buying a bunny!" Rudolph said. "I'm just saying that she's clearly a bunny-boiler, and that—"

"Oh, if she's going to make you a nice stew," said Chief Quim, "then that is a different matter altogether. Not much we can do about that, as upholders of the law, is there, Dufflecoat?"

The officer shook his head and then straightened his deerstalker. "Not if it's food-related," he said. "You want

Environmental Services for that, not out department." He prodded a finger into one ear and gave it a jolly good waggle. "All I can say is, if it's still pink in the middle at the point of service, ask to speak to the manager."

A madhouse! Rudolph thought. *I'm standing in the reception of a madhouse, conversing with its only two patients!*

"So that's it, is it?" said Rudolph. "Nothing can be done until—and it will happen, you mark my words—it is far too late?"

"Unless she actually does something," said Officer Dufflecoat, "our hands are completely tied."

"I have," said Chief Quim, "made a little note in this here notepad." He tapped it annoyingly with his pen. "Right underneath my picture of a hundred fatsos."

Had they known just what their money was paying for, taxpayers across the land would have asked for a complete refund, in full and with interest, but they were blissfully unaware, as is invariably the case in so many dimensions.

Rudolph left the police station dejected, bewildered, and fearful for what was yet to come. On top of that, his back was knackered from playing pack-mule all afternoon, and he'd

BABY RUDOLPH

picked up fleas from one of the non-magical reindeer at the zoo.

"Fuck!" he said, taking to the skies, where even the shoulder of a homeless swan was not enough to cry on.

15

As is often the case, night followed day. Rudolph sat at his computer, mashing at the keys with clumsy hoofs, nutting the mouse with his antlers, and generally pulling a face that would scare away even the most seasoned of crows.

He was pissed off.

Angry at the so-called justice system. And at Quim, personally, for persevering with that drawing gag, which hadn't got off to a good start, and then went downhill fast after that.

"There must be *som*ething," Rudolph said, right-clicking the mouse with one of his best stabbers.

He had been searching the Elfernet for almost three hours for something, *anything*, about how to deal with stalkers. This was the World Wide Web, so why was it so difficult to gather information about a certain subject and—

"Oh!" Rudolph said suddenly. "I've still got it on North Korea security settings!" He navigated to the cog icon, and then into the Settings section, where a toggle-switch of Kim Jong-Un's head stared out at him as if he'd just said something offensive about one his nuclear weapons. He clicked Un's head, and the Elfernet opened up to its full potential. Rudolph reproached himself thoroughly for the oversight, then got back to work.

"If you become romantically entangled with a fan of forest foreplay—"

Not that kind of stalking, for fuck's sake!

There were plenty of websites now; in fact, he was spoilt for choice. You *can* have too much of a good thing, it seemed, not that pages and pages of information about creepy creepers and stalky stalkers was a good thing (unless you are in training to become one, then fill your boots, it's all there, right down to which night-vision goggles are best for people with glaucoma and how long is too long when it comes to revealing that you've been living in the attic for the past six months?) but it was better than accidentally leaving your computer on psycho despot mode and having nothing at all.

"Living with your stalker," Rudolph said, in that slow, hypnotised, gormless way people do when reading aloud from a screen. "Never mind living with her," he said, suddenly snapping out of it. "I want her *gone*, no-fault-eviction, out of my life, thanks for the mammaries, ta-ta now."

There were whole websites from wannabe bestseller writers who had chosen stalking as a major plot-line in their next project and had decided to gift the entire dimension with not only a complete rundown of the story, but character profiles, AI images of what they might look like (if they had six fingers instead of the regulation three) and a playlist of songs that were being used to bring this nightmare scenario to life. *My last book reached 4,523 in the Stalker/Rapist/Summer Holiday Reads section, so let's get this one even higher, guys! Here's Coldplay with 'Yellow'.*

Rudolph was sick in his mouth, but swallowed it back down; egg-y, onion-y, cheese-y, it was like a blended quiche Lorainne, whatever that was.

His eyes fell upon something which looked promising; a thread, a talking board, or whatever you wanted to call it. He clicked the link and was taken to the site, where he discovered—

"I'll be fucking damned," he said.

There were dozens of folks here, all recounting their stalker-related troubles—some in rather terrifying detail, while others pussyfooted around the subject so gently that they eventually stopped talking altogether, exited the page, and went on to become clergy—and sharing tips on how to survive, should you, the reader, be experiencing the same, and even if you aren't, please read anyway, because we rely on clicks to pay for our hosting.

Rudolph scanned the list of threads until one, in particular, caught his eye.

e/mystalkerwantstoeatme

Call it whatever you want—morbid curiosity, a fascination for the macabre, the fact that he was getting nowhere fast, and at twice the speed, and so needed to ramp up his investigations before the sun came up and she, Merthyr, would be up and about, prowling the streets, sniffing him out with a picnic locked and loaded and an itinerary printed out—but Rudolph, before he realised he was going to, clicked it.

e/mystalkerwantstoeatme

I'm pretty sure my stalker wants to eat me, and I don't know what to do about it. This all started when I slept with her and woke up to find her, knife and fork in hand and eyeing up my bollocks. Please advise.

e/funnybastard80

Salt and pepper, tell her. Otherwise they just taste like cardboard.

e/livelaughlove

Maybe she was sleepwalking. You men think us women all psychos. Poor thing was probably in dreamland.

e/funnybastard80

Who put ten pence in you, livelaughlove? How does that help mystalkerwantstoeatme with his problem, starting with that nonsense?

e/mystalkerwantstoeatme

She wasn't asleep. Her eyes were proper wide, and she had a recipe book open on my chest.

e/funnybastard80

See, livelaughlove? Crazy bitch was looking at what to do with them, sauté or broil. An elf can't put up with that sort of crazy.

e/mystalkerwantstoeatme

When I asked her what she was doing, she completely flipped out on me, started asking me, "What kind of elf sleeps with cutlery and cookbooks under their pillow?"

e/funnybastard80

Classic gaslighting that, mate. Massive red flag. Glad you got out of there uneaten.

e/livelaughlove

While I'm happy you weren't cannibalised, I'm annoyed at yours and funnybastard80's continued assault on us females. This is why we choose the moose. You males are the reason we try to eat you in your sleep, so you only have yourselves to blame.

e/funnybastard80

Fucking hell, Sheila, give it a rest. He nearly got eaten in bed and you've made it all political.

e/mystalkerwantstoeatme

I think I'll be off now. Thanks for the help, guys.

e/funnybastard80

You're very welcome, mate.

e/livelaughlove

Oooh, "You're very welcome, mate," Get a room. I hear Andrew Tate's just opened a hotel. You'd love it there, you pair of absolute c...

END OF THREAD

Rudolph sighed and shook his head. This was getting him nowhere, and he was about to put a hoof through his computer screen when he saw, at the bottom of the thread he'd been reading, an advertisement.

Stalking is not the laughing matter it used to be. It's more

dangerous in 2024 than it ever has been before. Gone are the days of threatening love-letters and unwanted pizza deliveries. Our stalkers these days have knives, guns, and in some cases, even antlers. Our support group is here for you. We meet every second and fourth Wednesday of the month at Icy Lane Community Centre. 7pm sharp. Tea and coffee provided. Donations welcome. If you can't shake your stalker that day, please don't bother to turn up.

"Talk about a stroke of luck!" Rudolph said. "Because a moment ago, I was going to smash my computer screen and give up entirely, but now that I have seen this advertisement, the plot can further develop until it arrives at a suitable conclusion. It's almost ridiculous how that has happened." He turned to where a camera should have been and gave the empty space a knowing look.

Sarcastic bastard.

He'd made up his mind; tomorrow evening he would attend his first ever support group, see what all the fuss was about, and if nothing else, get his fill of free tea, coffee, and semi-stale biscuits.

16

Norm opened the pub at noon every day and had done since he'd taken over as landlord in the early eighteen-hundreds. Like clockwork, he was, and you could set your watch by him, so long as you didn't mind being five minutes either side of the correct time. Which was why it came as a complete shock when Finklefoot and Jimbo arrived at bang on noon to find the door wouldn't open, the curtains were still drawn, and two bottles of milk stood on the step like neglected, ginger stepchildren.

"Ah," said Finklefoot, putting on his monocle. "It would appear that we are early. Our hankering for ale has become such a problem that we are now officially amongst those strange creatures who hang about in front of pubs, knocking up the landlord, and demanding an immediate Hair of the Dog, or so help us, we'll leave a one-star review and ruin you!"

Jimbo shivered in the cold. It was snowing, for a change, "Maybe he died in his sleep," he said. "You know? It happens. He wasn't getting any younger."

Finklefoot considered this. Norm was somewhere in the region of eight-hundred years old, give or take five minutes either side, and one of the oldest elves Finklefoot knew that still had all his own teeth and at least one of his original hips. What were the odds that, after eight centuries alive, he should go to bed one night and die, without even a word of goodbye or a free pint to soften the blow? Once you got to that age, it was more of an effort to die than it was to just continue living.

"He's not dead," said Finklefoot, hefting his boot into the heavy pub door once again. "Put on your pince-nez, Jimbo. The game is afoot."

"The game is afoot? The ga... honestly, Eff-eff, that monocle has changed you. The game is afoot, indeed."

Finklefoot went round the back of The Partridge Inn, with Jimbo in tow, and gave that side of the pub a tickle with his boot, too. Jimbo watched in awe. *That's not how Sherlock would have done it*, he thought. *He'd have smoked some opium first, then got Watson to kick the door. Elementary.*

"Footprints!" said Finklefoot, pointing at the snow. "Leading from this rear entrance to somewhere over there." He pointed at the woods to the side of the pub. There was a

BABY RUDOLPH

thin, gossamer fog in the air, which made seeing that little bit trickier, but those footprints definitely went into the woods.

"Probably walking the dog," said Jimbo.

"Norm doesn't have a dog," Finklefoot replied. "And even if he did, he's not the type of fella that would walk it."

"Then he's bought a dog," said Jimbo, "and he's doing that thing all men do when they first get a dog, and giving it a good walk, the last good walk it'll ever have."

"I see only one fault in your reasoning," said Finklefoot.

"Which is?"

"No new doggy footprints." He pointed, once again, to the footprints in the snow. Just one pair of size twos, as dainty as you like.

"One of those little dogs that you carry in a pink handbag?" Jimbo said, for he was nothing if not resilient.

"What," said Finklefoot, rearing on his assistant, "is the point of having a dog and walking yourself? In other words, what kind of a sick, sociopathic sonofabitch buys a dog, sticks it in an Yves Saint Laurent, and goes hiking across the woodlands? At noon, no less, when there's a pub to open and punters waiting in the snow?"

Put like that, Jimbo thought, *it does seem a little odd.*

"Right!" Finklefoot said. "There's only one way to get to the bottom of it." He began to march towards the woods, stepping in whoever's prints as he went.

Jimbo followed, mainly because his colleague had promised to buy the first round, and he wasn't letting him out of his sight until he had.

They were roughly six trees deep when there came a grunt, a whistle, a pop, and a thunk, in that order and with very little time between.

Instinct took over, and Finklefoot dropped into an army-crawl and Jimbo shuffled up the nearest Aspen. A few seconds of silence passed, and then there was another grunt, whistle, pop, and thunk, which just went to show that the first one hadn't been a fluke.

Finklefoot rolled onto his back and searched, momentarily confused, for his assistant. A sudden movement from the top of a nearby tree caught his eye, and he sighed heavily and rolled his eyes. *What the fuck are you doing up there?* he mouthed.

Jimbo must not have understood, because he replied with a thumbs-up and a nod that said, *Thanks! It was all my own idea!*

Grunt-whistle-pop-thunk.

BABY RUDOLPH

What in the name of seven lords a-leapin' is making that noise? he mouthed. If his friend had struggled with translating his first question, he had no chance at all with this one. Finklefoot's suspicions were confirmed when Jimbo made the universal sign of *Can't understand a fucking word of it, mate*, followed by a shrug powerful enough to almost topple him from the tree.

Get down here, Finklefoot mouthed, and gestured, also.

Jimbo understood that one, and began to descend the tree. He fell the last two feet and disappeared into a snow flurry at the tree's base.

"What is that noise?" Finklefoot asked as Jimbo finally arrived at his side, covered in snow, and looking like something a dog does in winter.

"Never heard anything like it before," whispered Jimbo. "But it has to be Norm, doesn't it?"

Finklefoot nodded. As much as it bothered him, once you eliminate the impossible, whatever remains, no matter how improbable, must be the truth. Conan Doyle had a way with words that Finklefoot didn't. "It's definitely Norm, the cunt," he said to Jimbo. "Has to be. The prints don't lie."

"Shakira?" Jimbo said.

"What?"

"Never mind." Jimbo got to his feet and dusted most of the snow from his person. "Come on, then," he said. "If it's Norm, there's nothing to worry about. He's a mate of ours—"

"A mate who's just started going grunt-whistle-pop-thunk!" Finklefoot said. "He never *used* to do that."

Jimbo clipped his pince-nez into place and took the lead. Finklefoot rushed to his feet and shuffled after him, wondering how the power had shifted so quickly, and how best to get it back without dying first.

He needn't have worried, because a moment later they stepped into a clearing just in time to find Norm and the source of that ridiculous noise.

The clearing had been converted into an arena, of sorts, only one without seats and hot-dog vendors and, Finklefoot was rather sad to see, cheerleaders throwing themselves about the place. Apart from that, though, it was remarkably arena-like.

There was something odd about this arena, though, in that there was a little person stood in the middle of it with a great bloody big bow that would have made Legolas cream himself. Surrounding this elf on all sides were homemade archery targets. You could tell they were homemade because one of them looked like an ironing board, one bore an uncanny resemblance to a mahogany dining-room table, and another looked just like the old front door of the pub, which had been kicked off by the licensing committee one Sunday night to break up what had been a relatively harmless lock-in.

Coloured balloons were attached to these objects, some of which had already been burst by arrows.

Norm, for it was he at the centre of this magnificent theatre in the woods, nocked an arrow, gave it a jolly good pull back, and let go with a grunt.

Grunt-whistle-pop-thunk.

"Ah!" said Finklefoot. "Makes sense when you actually watch it happen!"

Upon hearing this, Norm spun so quickly, had an arrow ready to release, that Finklefoot thought, *He's wasted as a landlord*, before throwing himself to the snow and hoping the arrow sailed harmlessly between his arse cheeks.

"It's just us!" Jimbo said, throwing his arms into the air. "Your number one patrons!"

Norm frowned, keeping the arrow trained on them, as if he wasn't quite sure if he believed that they were who they said they were, or if he did, he already had the arrow nocked and it would be a shame not to let it fly now.

Finklefoot slowly gathered his limbs and got back to his feet. "Fucking hell, Norm, what's all this, then?" He made an all-encompassing gesture to the clearing. "It's a bit late for the Olympics, but another one'll be along in roughly three years."

Shame seemed to wash over Norm, and he lowered the bow and popped the arrow back into a quiver hanging from his belt. He looked, to all intents and purposes, like an elf who had been caught doing something he shouldn't have. The face of a bloke whose wife has just come home early and caught him with his trousers around his ankles, a vacuum cleaner in one hand and a can of WD40 in the other.

"I wasn't doing nothing," Norm said as he slowly walked towards them.

"You bloody well were," said Jimbo. "You were training for *The Hunger Games*, you were."

Finklefoot said, "I didn't know you were an archer, Norm. And a damn good one, by the looks of it."

Norm shrugged. His cheeks were flushed with embarrassment, his eyes were wide, as if pleading with them not to tell anyone what he got up to when no one was looking. "It's nothing," he said. "Just something I like to do before opening up bang on time."

BABY RUDOLPH

Finklefoot checked his watch. "If you're planning on opening up, bang on time, I suggest you invent a time-machine, pop back to this time, five minutes ago, and be at the door with the key in the lock and your little hand giving it a gentle turn to the right."

Norm checked his own watch. "Bloody thing," he said. "It's usually right, give or take five minutes."

"Shall we continue this discussion across the bar, where it's warm and there is a beer in my hand?" Finklefoot said.

"Probably a warm beer," added Jimbo.

"I shall put an arrow in you," said Norm.

Once inside, and the removal of pointy hats and coats had occurred, Finklefoot and Jimbo assumed their usual spots at the bar and Norm affected the position of barman-cum-landlord, as he had done thousands of times before. Two pints of 'the usual' were poured, and Norm fixed himself a large Scotch, no ice, no water, the way it should, in his opinion, always be served and consumed.

"So, let me get this straight," said Finklefoot, scraping the massive head from his ale with a beer-mat. "You're an archer?"

Norm sighed, as if he'd not only wanted to draw a line under the subject, but also fold it up, pop it into an envelope, and toss it into Mount Doom.

"Have you ever heard of the Classified Brotherhood of Licensee Archers?" Norm asked, necking his Scotch and replenishing his glass.

"No," said Finklefoot. "Is it like Fight Club? Because if it is, you really shouldn't be talking about it."

"The CBLA is—"

"Now you can't go making acronyms up, willy-nilly," Jimbo said. "And as far as they go, that one sounds like something that prevents you from driving if you've defaulted on your alimony."

Norm picked up the little knife he uses to cut lemons into quarters and gave Jimbo a look.

"You were saying..." said Jimbo with a squeak.

The landlord put the knife down and went on. "Well, we used to just be a darts league," he said. "You know, head-to-heads once a week, major tourney four times a year, scoreboards and the like? Well, us landlords got bored of all that, and sick of the after-match brawls between rival pubs, because nothing hits harder than a landlord outscored. We decided there was no honour in darts anymore, and to be quite frank, no one was coming to the matches anyway." He began filling the peanut bowls and setting them out on the bar as he continued to speak.

BABY RUDOLPH

Finklefoot yawned and wished he'd never asked, now.

"We decided, us licensees, that if no one was gonna come and watch us play darts, they might as well not come and watch us doing archery, which if you think about it is just darts but with bigger arrows and balloons instead of treble-twenties.

"So, the CBLA started, and it was good fun, to begin with. We were all about as shit as each other, and you'd be lucky if you got out of there with your extremities intact and your bollocks un-punctured. The Classified Brotherhood of Licensee Archers became a registered business, only because it was classified, we didn't tell anyone that it was registered, not even the authorities, and certainly not the taxman."

"It wasn't," said Finklefoot, "registered at all, then?"

"Nah. Couldn't be arsed with all the paperwork," Norm said. "But we told other licensees it was, and they believed us, because they were drunk half the time, the way we usually are, and would have believed it if we'd told them up was down and that if you stare at a parrot for long enough, it'll just explode through sheer paranoia."

"Which you obviously did," said Jimbo.

Norm nodded. "And then," he said, "it all started to go wrong for the CBLA. Folks just stopped turning up to the meetings, on account of their sudden and mysterious deaths from centuries of alcohol abuse, and in the end there was just me. It's been that way ever since."

"And you've just kept on going?" said Finklefoot, cleaning his monocle with his mitten. Norm nodded again. "That's one of the saddest things I've ever heard. Pint of 'same again', hold the ice-cream."

"The thing is," Norm went on as he poured Finklefoot's 'same again', "I got really good at it. These past few decades, I find it more difficult to miss on purpose than to pop those bloody balloons. I'm the last surviving member of the Classified Brotherhood of Licensee Archers, and I'm going to show everyone what it's all about."

Finklefoot pushed his monocle into place and said, "Oh, here we go. This is the bit when you tell us you're taking part in the Land of Christmas Annual Variety Show this weekend."

"Oh, please don't tell us *that*," said Jimbo. "Our *Bee Gees* tribute won't stand a chance against your arrow bullshit."

"Well," said Norm, "I wasn't gonna get involved, you know? But then I realised everyone else was doing something. Hattie Quim's choir, Shart's Incredible Stabbing Cutlery, Rudolph's stand-up, your *Bee Gees* thing, Jessica Claus's slippery tuna pole routine... I just felt like I had to do something."

"There is no *Bee Gees* thing," Finklefoot said, for he was still of the opinion that getting up and embarrassing himself in front of thousands of denizens of the Land of Christmas would not look good on his resume, and since the prize for coming first was that you got to switch on the Christmas lights come December the first—lights which were on all year round anyway, so the whole thing was just a charade and a ploy to sell overpriced bratwurst, piss-warm wine, and little automaton toys that were destined to break down before New Year—it really wasn't worth getting out of bed for.

With Norm out of earshot, and as if that made any kind of difference in the slightest, Jimbo turned on his stool and surreptitiously said, "What's the plan for today, Eff-eff?"

"Why are you whispering like that? Why on earth are you talking from the corner of your mouth as if you've suffered a stroke? We have nothing to hide, Jimbo, because we know nothing, and even if we did, it wouldn't be a secret."

"Fair enough," said Jimbo. "But we *do* know something, though. We've got some evidence."

Finklefoot considered this; yesterday, upon discovering the little object of possible importance, he had been excited, elated, and dare he say it, inexplicably aroused. One step closer to finding Ahora, dead or alive (but probably dead) and within touching distance of bringing the responsible fiend to justice, where he would face the full force of the criminal justice system, and probably get off on a technicality.

That had been yesterday. Today was a different day to yesterday, hence the name change, and a lot of things had happened since stumbling, fortuitously, upon that possible piece of evidence in the alleyway.

For starters, it had occurred to Finklefoot, whilst he had been writhing around on top of his beloved and trying to find a hole that would stay still for long enough for him to slip it home, that elves do not have fingerprints.

"What's the matter, dear?" Trixie had asked, bringing a halt to his sexy struggles. "It's okay," she'd gone on. "It happens to every elf now and then. Probably too much ale, that's all. I'll be open again tomorrow night."

"Elves don't have fingerprints!" he'd yelled into the side of her disappointed face. "It's useless, inadmissible in court, might as well throw it away!"

"Quite so, dear," his wife had said, sliding from beneath him like an octopus abandoning ship.

BABY RUDOLPH

She hadn't understood and had spent the rest of the night in the bathroom finishing herself off.

"That piece of evidence," said Finklefoot to Jimbo, "is useless. It is about as useful as brakes on a hand-glider. We do not have the requisite friction ridges in our fingers to leave a mark on the things we touch. Therefore, we do not have those little scanner machines at the station to press our digits and palms against when we've done something naughty, and thus, there is no database we can sit in front of and watch the images of all the criminals of the Land whizz by at breakneck speed until a match is found and we can nail this sick sonofabitch. We have nothing to go on, apart from a rag which smells faintly of chloroform and that little plastic thing we're not mentioning yet!" He inhaled sharply and added, "So today's plan will mostly consist of getting very drunk, wallowing in self-pity, absolutely NOT talking about the *Bee Gees* or archery, and trying to figure out why my little elf-cock does not work half as well as it used to!"

"Have you ever considered therapy?" said Jimbo, finishing his ale and ordering another with the customary raised finger.

And so it was that the rest of the afternoon was spent mixing Scotch and Ale at the bar in The Partridge Inn. At some point—it could have taken a minute, or an hour, time was no longer relevant to Finklefoot and Jimbo, who were off work and putting two and two together in the most unfeasible of ways—the place had filled up.

"When," slurred Finklefoot, "did all these fuckers come in?"

"Must be after five," replied Jimbo, the pince-nez balancing on the bridge of his nose askew and relatively useless. "We really should be looking for Ahora," he went on, "or at least appearing to be looking."

Finklefoot munched down on a pretzel. "You know what your problem is?" he said, swaying unsteadily on his stool. Being an elf, it was a long way to the ground, and the vertiginous view, coupled with the double-vision brought on by too much booze, was starting to cause him problems.

"My wife," said Jimbo, "says it's how I always leave things until the last minute, then get all flustered trying to get them done."

"No," said Finklefoot. "Your problem is... I've forgotten now, but it was a problem a moment ago, and not much has happened since then, so sort your life out, because it's mildly annoying, whatever it is."

"Same again?" Norm said, appearing at their end of the bar like a ninja with a stopwatch.

"We'll have two pi—"

"I think we've had enough," Jimbo interrupted, which, judging by the expression his friend had affected, might very well be the problem Finklefoot had been referring to. "We'll end up in cells, if we continue at this rate."

Finklefoot steadied himself with the help of the bar, and held up a finger. All covered in bits of pretzel, it was. His face was that of an elf whose confusion had been suddenly dispersed by the arrival of a cartoon lightbulb, which now hovered above his head, forty watts of genius.

"That's it!" he said. "He'll know what to do next. He's an evil bastard, but if I take him something, he'll point us in the right direction."

"What the hell are you talking about, man?" Jimbo asked, firmly.

Finklefoot was too busy filling his pockets with bar snacks to hear the question, and when he leapt down off the stool he staggered back and forth momentarily, as if this was his first time experiencing gravity; give him a few moments to get to grips with it, because no one rushed Neil Armstrong when he did it.

Jimbo went and put his hat and coat on. It appeared that they were leaving.

"Now, if I could just remember where I put my car keys..." said Finklefoot, searching all around and about him.

"We didn't drive here," said Jimbo. "In fact," he went on, "*no one* drives here."

"That'll be why I can't find them, then."

Jimbo thanked Norm for his hospitality and both he and Finklefoot made their way toward the exit, bouncing off each other, the fruit machine, two geriatric ex-boxers who took it personally, and then the door frame.

The door hit them both in the arses on their way out.

17

There is no Aurora Borealis in the Land of Christmas, and no Aurora Australis, either. This is because it exists in an entirely different dimension to earth, one not too far distant, but you'd have trouble walking it, and you couldn't have your mail redirected there. The Land of Christmas had its own natural light show, in the form of Aurora Bora Bora Sayonara, whose magnificence can not be put into words, which is a shame, really, because you would have liked it. It was through Aurora Bora Bora Sayonara that Rudolph now flew on his way to the community centre in Icy Lane, and he was both nervous and anxious to get it over with.

That afternoon had come a barrage of new messages from Merthyr. Hundreds of them, all misspelt, all angry or horny or both, all signed off with some variation of SNET FROM ELF-FON. He'd read through them, trembling, in disbelief, and wishing he was one of the non-magical reindeer at the zoo, who didn't know how lucky they were that all they had to worry about was being overfed by excited children.

They wouldn't last a *day* in my hooves.

The messages from Merthyr had become so unhinged toward the end that even Rudolph's computer had started to hiss and smoke, and he'd had to cool it down with a bucket of water and a gentle reading of *Sonnet 18*.

Shall I compare thee to a summer's day…?

Shakespeare had no idea what he was babbling on about. Love, the love that Rudolph was learning about now, did not involve summer days.

Thou art more lovely and more temperate…

The love that Rudolph was discovering did not go that way at all. More like, *Shall I compare ye to a wee basket of treacle… thou are more thick but still slip through the gaps, ye wee shite.*

In a way, Merthyr was something of a poet. Her messages always contained words Rudolph didn't know, and she spoke in some weird, obfuscating half-language that made it difficult to know whether she was being nice or if she really *was* going to put him in a sandwich and feed him to the ducks.

Rough winds do shake the darling buds of May…

In Merthyr-speak, that would be, *My farts are so bad, I can rattle the wee conkers out of trees from three-hundred yards.* It didn't have quite the same beautiful ring to it. But poetry, like most things, is subjective, and one man's Keats is another man's Will Smith, or something along those lines.

"You are arriving at your destination," said the device strapped to Rudolph's ankle. "How many stars would you rate the free version of this app on a scale of—"

Rudolph clicked it off and prepared to land.

Once on the ground, the realisation of what he was about to do truly hit home. As he slowly walked toward the community centre's entrance, its bright yellow lights about as welcoming as a British naval boat intercepting a rubber dinghy, he tried to justify Merthyr's behaviour, because if she wasn't stalking him and making his life a living nightmare, then he wouldn't have to go in there and tell strangers all about it. So, she's sent you more than five-hundred messages of madness in the past forty-eight hours; who doesn't do that when they're excited? So, she talks like she wants to kiss him one minute, and then bite his nose off the next; who doesn't have highs and lows and good days and bad?

The more he tried to justify it, though, the more he realised Merthyr was stark staring bonkers, and he needed help, or at least some advice, on how to deal with it without ending up in several pieces, scattered about the snowy beaches, and wishing someone would come along soon and put him back together, because the cold was playing havoc with his exposed nerves and his head always felt better when it had something to stand on.

He nudged the community centre door open with his nose and found himself in a foyer. The kind of area reserved for doctor's surgeries, community centres, and Citizen's Advice Bureaus, all blue carpet, cream walls, and the smell of lemon Pledge hanging heavily in the air.

Directly in front was a set of double-doors, upon which someone had Sellotaped a piece of paper identifying it as the door leading to the Survivors of Stalkers meeting. It also said that they had to be out before nine, as it was Karate tonight, and no one from the group was really up for a fight.

Rudolph entered and was immediately surprised at the turnout. He counted seven elves in total, and assuming only one of them ran the show, that meant six of them were in the same predicament as him.

"Haven't seen you here before," said an elf as Rudolph attempted to make a coffee at the edge of the room, where the table with the biscuits and the drinks-making facilities had been set up.

"First time," Rudolph said, suddenly feeling very conspicuous.

BABY RUDOLPH

"I'm Roger," the elf said in a higher-than-usual helium-voice. "That's not my real name, of course. Had to change it for obvious reasons, but that's the name I go by now."

Rudolph told him that it was a nice name—a harmless lie; who goes by Roger these days?—and could he please help with the milk, because Rudolph had had trouble getting the top off.

"You'll be fine," Roger told him. "They're all nice here. No judgment, you know? We're all in the same boat."

"Up Shit Creek without a paddle?" Rudolph said before he'd had time to think about it.

"There is a paddle," Roger said. "You just need to know where to find it so that you can steer yourself back on course."

Fuck! thought Rudolph. *One of those kinds of meeting, is it?* He was about to empty his coffee into the sink, put the biscuit plate down, and head for the exit when SHE came through it. Not Merthyr, of course, that would be utterly terrifying. No, this was the *opposite* of Merthyr. Well, visually it was. A female reindeer—a cow so resplendent that Rudolph's knees buckled and fifteen chocolate Hob Nobs headed for the carpet.

She was stunning, if you like that sort of thing, and as she moved across the room, Rudolph could have sworn he heard angels singing.

"Put your tongue away, dickhead," squeaked Roger. "It's a survivor's group, not speed-dating."

The meeting started as they invariably do, with everyone saying their names and that yes, they were also being stalked, hounded, bombarded, and pursued by unwanted beings. Rudolph didn't see the point of it, of course, since they were all using fake names and it said on the door exactly why they were there. In his opinion, they could have skipped that bit entirely and gone on to the heart-rending misery. He went with the flow, though, gave his name (under severe pressure) and now had to go the rest of the night being called Jasper, for fuck's sake.

It turned out that their stories and experiences were varied. Some were just being plagued by love-letters and Adele mixtapes, others were at their wit's end and sick of receiving elf heads in the post. When it came to Rudolph's turn to speak, he had a good idea he was somewhere between the two extremes.

"So, tell us, Jasper," said Cort, the leader of the group. Rudolph winced at the sound of his new name. "Been having some problems in the whole 'unwanted attention' department, have we?"

Understatements like that usually don't come with a smile and a happy clap, but this one did. Cort, it seemed, enjoyed his job a little too much.

"You could say that," said Rudolph, setting his too-hot coffee down next to his seat. "My stalker, Me—"

"We don't use their names in here," Cort said suddenly. "It gives them power, you see. Using their name makes them stronger. We just use pronouns."

Fair enough, Rudolph thought, although he couldn't get his head around how it gave them power, unless they knew about the meetings and were waiting outside with a rolled-up newspaper.

"My stalker, she's sending me messages, hundreds of them, one after another. Not that I want to respond to them, but I couldn't if I wanted to. She changes subjects quicker than *Mastermind*."

"We try to limit the number of witty similes we use during meetings," said Cort. "But I'll give you that one for free."

Rudolph fought back the urge to low-kick the little shit from his chair and went on. "I went out with her once—"

A collective chorus of breath intakes almost sucked Rudolph out of his chair. The temperature in the room seemed to drop by about two degrees.

"What?" said Rudolph. "Did I say something weird?"

Cort leaned forward in his chair and knitted his little hands together. "You're not supposed to go out with them," he said. "Makes a stalker-victim relationship into an *actual* relationship."

"I was scared of her," Rudolph said. "Of what she would do to me if I told her no."

All around the room there were nods; the beautiful reindeer whose fake name was Wish made eye-contact with him for the first time. If fireworks were allowed to be set up in such a confined space, now would have been the time they went off.

"Do you *regret* this date with your stalker?" asked Cort, who was really starting to get on Rudolph's tits. "Or perhaps you enjoyed it, in some sick, erotic way. Are you a pervert, Jasper?"

Rudolph picked his coffee cup up from the carpet. It would, he thought, make an interesting projectile, should Cort continue with his current line of questioning. The old saying went: You can soak an elf in hot coffee, but he'll always be screaming too much to drink.

"I didn't enjoy *anything* about it," said Rudolph, which was sort of a lie, as he'd never done clay penguin shooting before and he found it rather cathartic. "It was a nightmare from start to finish. I'd only gone there so she wouldn't beat me up. I thought it might satisfy her for a while, you know? Give her a little fix of Ru..." He quickly stopped himself. "Taste of *Jasper*," he corrected. "And that would be enough and make her go away. But she's worse than ever! You should see some of the things she wants to do to me. I'm not even bodily capable of half of them. What's a 'forward-roll sixty-nine with rice', anyway? I haven't a bloody clue, but *she* does. *She* knows all the positions, most of which sound illegal, and all of which she'll have to do on her own, because I'm not gonna fucking be there for it! This carries on, I'm moving to the Realm of Hanukkah, changing my name by deed poll—" not to Jasper, though, "—and becoming a monk."

"Running away from your problems will not make them go away," Cort said in that strange manner he had of making absolutely no sense at all. "Until you come to terms with the fact that you, Jasper, are a stalkee, and accept that you will *always* be a stalkee, no matter how far you run or how well you hide, you're only lying to yourself."

Rudolph was confused, and his face said as much. What a strange meeting this was turning out to be. Part of him had started to think he would have been better off joining the 9pm Karate group instead; at least he could have learnt a thing or two about how to batter a big bitch of a cow. Instead he was here, listening to the Dalai Loony witter endlessly on with adages that had never seen a proofreader, let alone made it across an editor's desk.

"I know what you're going through," said Wish, and Rudolph's massive reindeer cock suddenly proudly saluted, and he quickly crossed his legs and hoped that no one had noticed. There was just something so demure, delightful, and downright delectable about her voice; it was like treacle strained through a solid-gold colander. She had a voice for radio, and her face wasn't anything to sniff at, either, though Rudolph hoped he could at some point in the near future.

"You do?" said Rudolph, sounding like a child who's just been told by his parents that they know where they're going on holiday this year.

Wish nodded. "I thought the same about *my* stalker," she said. "That if I went out with them once, and made it a complete nightmare, it would put them off." She ran a well-manicured hoof through her hair and went on. "It didn't. No matter how much of an idiot I made myself, it didn't work. They were into it. Even called me a 'wee stupid-but-sexy fairground goldfish, and dinnae dare grow a wee big heed 'bout it!'"

Rudolph's erection packed two suitcases, locked all the doors on the way out, and boarded the next available flight to Peru.

"What was that?" he said, for he must have misheard. Long sleepless nights, that's what it was. That and all the worry, quite right.

"Wee sexy fairground goldfish?" Wish said. It was her turn to look confused, and she was particularly good at it. "Something wrong, Jasper?" she said. "You look like you've seen a ghost."

And he did. He'd turned a strange off-brown colour, and his eyes were like saucers. If he was trying to impress Wish, who was looking at him with all the concern of a mother witnessing their child come down a slide unaided for the very first time, he was going about it the wrong way.

"That's more than enough impressions for one night," Cort said. "It's not nice to imitate one's stalker, especially when they're not here to follow us home."

After a few moments, Rudolph managed to speak. "I believe Wish and I have experienced something similar," he said. His throat felt as if it had been coated with asphalt and then glass, and once the glass had been put down, gone over with a steamroller.

"That's what these meetings are all about," said Cort, leaning back in his chair as if to say, *See? Didn't I tell you I was brilliant? You're welcome!* "Even though we are all broken, terrified, paranoid shells of our former selves, with no one else to turn to because we've isolated ourselves from this world and from our families and friends, all thanks to our stalkers, solace can always be found of a Wednesday evening at Icy Lane Community Centre." He clapped his little hands together; this prick, Rudolph thought, had definitely been a milk monitor at school.

As the meeting wound down—an angry elf in a white karate Gi was putting his boot into the door and shouting something in ersatz Japanese—the stalkees, as Cort liked to call them, left the building in that special way only people who are used to being followed can: neck on a swivel, like an owl on acid, and doing that odd little walk-run, walk-run thing, as if it might throw off any potential stalkers, or at least leave them confused.

Rudolph waited outside in the snow.

Wish trotted out of the building, and was in the process of wrapping a scarf round her neck when—

"Can I have a word?" Rudolph said, or would have had he managed to get the words out in time.

But there hadn't been time. Wish had plunged a hoof into her handbag, pulled out the mace, and was spraying it in his eyes and face, ironically before he'd managed to reach "I". She continued to spray as she fumbled about with a rape alarm.

"It's me!" Rudolph spluttered as he took a step back. "Jasper! It's Jasper!"

She stopped spraying and gave him a look. Of course, Rudolph couldn't see this look, because he'd just been pepper-sprayed directly into the eyeballs, but he imagined she was frowning slightly, and hopefully had the common decency to show some remorse.

"Jasper!" she said, dropping the mace into her handbag. "You scared the droppings out of me. I'm so sorry, just an old habit, I guess, and you know what they say about old habits."

Rudolph blinked and blinked. "They sting like a motherfucker?" he said. "Honestly, where did you even get mace from in the Land of Christmas? Goddammit, it hurts so bad. Fuck!"

"I make it myself," said Wish. At least it sounded like Wish. For all he knew, she'd done a runner and left her voice to do the explaining. "Got gallons of the stuff at home. You can never be too careful; I learned that the hard way." She produced a gingham hankie from her bag, gave it a little Hawk Tuah—whatever the fuck that was—and began to wipe in and around Rudolph's eyes. "Why did you say your name was Jasper?" she asked.

"Because," said Rudolph, enjoying the relief of the gingham hankie, "that's my name. Jasper. Jasper Carrot."

"Your name is not Jasper Carrot," laughed Wish. "You're Rudolph. The bloody big, red nose is a dead giveaway."

"I forgot about that," Rudolph said. He could see something now. A face, a gingham hankie, blurry but promising. He wasn't going to lose his eyesight, after all. "You know when you get used to your strange bits and bobs, your warts and freckles, not that you have any, you're perfect, but you do, you get used to them and forget they're even there after a while." Was he making any sense at all? He wasn't sure. "At least, that's what I'm like with my nose."

Wish had finished wiping mace from his eyes and screwed the hankie up, popped it into her handbag, and said, "Really? Is that why I saw the Hunchback walking round Tesco's this morning?"

"You never did," Rudolph said, and then quickly added, "Oh, fuck, you were joking. Of course you were."

"Right," she said. "I think I managed to get most of it out, but you might want to soak it in warm water when you get home."

"I will," said Rudolph, and then it occurred to him, the reason he'd been pepper-sprayed in the first place. He'd wanted to ask her something, and so he did. "Er, Wish, I think, well, I might need your advice, and I, er..." He couldn't tell her that he believed they shared a stalker; no one likes sharing, not even reindeer. "Would you meet me, say, tomorrow? Lunchtime in The Paddock Arms? I'll hopefully be able to focus on you better then, without all the blinking and eye-streaming."

Wish told him that yes, that would be fine, and that he should perhaps wear a distinguishing object, a red rose, or a jester's hat, something to prove he is who he says he is, otherwise there's a relatively small chance he'll find himself with a faceful of mace once again.

"I'm joking about the jester's hat," she said with a laugh. "You've got a massive red hooter, for fuck's sake! That's like putting an alarm clock on a fire-engine."

There are times in life when you're not sure whether you're being insulted or not, and it's during these times you find yourself simply nodding along, laughing a little, and trying not to think about it too deeply.

That's what Rudolph was doing. He was still doing it when—

"See you tomorrow, then," Wish said, and took to a run, which turned into a flight, and as Rudolph watched her silhouette grow smaller and smaller against the Aurora Bora Bora Sayonara, he realised he was smiling.

When was the last time he'd really smiled? For the life of him, he couldn't remember, but it must have been a while because he was apparently rusty, and it hurt more than it should have. Like someone wedging a coat-hanger into his cheeks.

He walked round the outside of the community centre; inside, he could hear the collective "Oss, Senseis!" of thirty elf martial artists, and was suddenly glad he'd gone to the meeting, after all, for if he hadn't, then he'd never have met Wish—he would try to coax her real name out of her tomorrow, but he rather liked Wish—and he'd never have heard about her experiences with, what had to be, Merthyr Titful. How many other stalkers spoke like that? *Wee* this and *dinnae* that, it had to be Merthyr. He'd put money on it if he weren't saving for a non-snowy day.

He took off and flew for home, completely unaware that one of his worst nightmares—not the one with the school play and the diaper, nor the one where all his teeth fell out and when they came back through, surprise, surprise, fucking popcorn!—was waiting for him.

*

Snow was coming down in sheets; as already ascertained, nothing out of the ordinary. You could expect snow as readily as you might your next breath. That didn't mean it wasn't a pain in the backside when you were a creature—or two creatures, in this case—no taller than your average three-year-old human, and you were trying to get somewhere in a hurry.

"I can't see where I'm going!" Jimbo called out into the void, hoping that the only voice that came back belonged to his boss, his long-time friend, and as of half an hour ago during a rather drunken discussion, the registered owner of FF&J Investigations.

"Almost there, Gizmo!" came the reply, which was not a good sign.

"It's Jimbo!" he called back. "Who the fuck is Gizmo?"

"You'll have to shout louder!" said Finklefoot, trying to out-roar the storm, and somehow coming third. "I can't see a bloody thing! Did we end up in the park again?"

They had hoped the cold would sober them up, but after leaving the pub, a conversation with a strangely well-mannered bicycle had put things into perspective, and so they had spent the last two hours zig-zagging through the snow, occasionally stopping for a little lie down, and discussing such wondrous things as the Aurora Bora Bora Sayonara, the mortality of humans, why toast always lands butter side down, and how many clowns you could really fit into a Mini Cooper, if you were to really stuff them in.

A light suddenly came slowly into view, and Jimbo thought somewhat selfishly, *Just walk into it. You've always wanted to meet God, so now's your chance...*

BABY RUDOLPH

It turned out to be, not the hallway to Heaven, but the LCPD station they'd been trying to find for the best part of the night. Jimbo was somewhat disappointed; he'd heard the croissants in Heaven were sublime.

"See?" Finklefoot slurred, dusting a foot of snow from his hat, and shaking the rest off like a Shih-Tzu coming in out of the rain. "Told you I knew where I was going."

"Is that why you stopped to ask that postbox for directions?"

"Well, we're here now, and I'll bet our friends Chief Quim and Officer Dufflecoat will fight each other over which one of them gets to put the kettle on for us."

Jimbo dusted himself down, wrung out his hat and beard, and told Finklefoot what he'd like to do with a kettle, and it involved turning it sideways.

"No need to be like that," said Finklefoot, pushing the door which would lead into the police station.

Would lead.

As in, it *would* have done, had the thing not put up such a fight and decided to stay shut instead.

Finklefoot turned to face Jimbo, whose face was a picture, and that picture was *The Great Day of His Wrath* by

John Martin. "It appears to be shut," Finklefoot said, eyes rolling drunkenly in their sockets.

Jimbo pushed him out of the way, stuck on his pince-nez, and peered at the sign hanging on the inside of the door: Opening Hours — 9am - 9pm Monday-Friday. Shut on Weekends — No Loitering — No Heavy Petting — Please Don't Feed the Animals.

Jimbo gave his watch a cursory glance, saw that it offered nothing but unwelcome news, and decided to clobber Finklefoot with his wet hat instead. "You fucking prick!" he said. "It closed five minutes ago!"

Finklefoot snatched the wet hat out of Jimbo's hands and hit him back. "It's not my fault, you little bastard!"

Jimbo took the hat back, straightened it out, and then hit Finklefoot with it once more. "Whose fault is it, then? The postbox's?"

"Fucking *Norm*'s fault!" said Finklefoot, trying to have his go with the hat, but Jimbo was too quick and put it on his head.

"How, great leader, is this in any way, shape or form, Norm's fault?" He folded his arms churlishly across his chest and waited for a reply. He didn't have to wait too long, just enough time for Finklefoot to fold his inebriated tongue around the words trying to run away from him.

"Well, of course it was Norm's fault," he said. "I mean, if he'd have opened up on time, everything would have been nudged back five minutes, wouldn't it?" He held out his hands as if to say, *Ta-Da! A reason! Like it or lump it.*

"Bollocks!" Jimbo said. "That makes no sense at all."

"It really does if you don't think about it too hard," said Finklefoot. "If Norm had opened up bang on Noon, we'd have started drinking by one-past. We would have got through all that stuff about the archery, all that stuff with my existential crisis, your *genius thinking—*" he really pronounced those last two words hard, because if there was one thing Finklefoot knew how to do, it was butter up an idiot "—about coming to the station to have a word with you-know-who, all of that would have happened five minutes earlier. We'd have left the pub, still pissed as farts, five minutes earlier, and staggered about in the snow for two hours, but we'd still have arrived here precisely five minutes ago, when this place was still open, and Quim would have made us a nice cup of coffee and..." He trailed off there and his mouth fell open, as if someone had popped a couple of fingers up him when he wasn't looking. "We've travelled into the future!"

"Oh, for fuck's sake!" Jimbo said, stepping back down into the snow. There were two steps, and he forgot about at least one of them, but when he picked himself back up, he said, "I'm going home to the missus."

"Oh, come on, Jim... Jimb... I'm thinking *Gizmo* suits you better—"

"Bye, Eff-eff!"

"Look," said Finklefoot, "we can't very well call it a night now. We've come all this way, and Ahora still hasn't turned up dead, so..." He left it at that; surely it was enough.

Jimbo stopped walking and turned. "Please accept my resignation from FF&J Investigations. I'll have it in writing and on your desk by mor—"

"Resignation?" said Finklefoot, looking like someone who'd just lot a fiver and found a cockroach. "We've only been going twenty minutes."

"I know," said Jimbo, "but my heart's not in it anymore." He turned and started to walk again, but didn't get far before s shadow fell upon him.

"Double-yew-tee-fuck," Finklefoot said, for the shadow had also fallen upon him.

BABY RUDOLPH

They both looked up, and as if some *deus ex-machina* had appeared in the sky above and was about to change everything for purposes of plot continuation.

"Rudolph?" said Jimbo.

"Rudy!" said Finklefoot.

The magical reindeer, red nose alight and flashing intermittently like an arriving AA van, hovered above, blocking out the moon. It was all very cinematic, and probably would have done better box office had Rudolph been wearing a cape.

"Anything I can help with?" said the reindeer. "I was just on my way home, saw you two, and I thought, Now there're two elves who could use some assistance."

Jimbo made his way back to Finklefoot's side. "Ask him," he said. "He's the one who's got us into this mess."

"Bloody have not," Finklefoot said, firmly. "Rudy, is there any chance you could help us get into the police station? I'm not talking about breaking and entering here. Just entering will do."

Rudolph looked down at the station, and then back at the two elves. "Piece of piss," he said. "I'll do a drive-by and leave you two to it."

Finklefoot looked at Jimbo.

Jimbo looked at Finklefoot.

Rudolph was already swooping around the building, preparatory to doing whatever it was he was about to do.

"Don't hurt it!" Jimbo called up to Rudolph, but the reindeer either didn't hear him, or did, and chose not to listen. Either way, the effect was the same.

What happened next was nothing short of a miracle. Of course, this is Rudolph we're talking about, but that didn't make it any less spectacular. After taking a run-up (fly-up?) of around a hundred metres, the reindeer began to fly, full-pelt, toward the airspace above the police station. He covered the distance in less than two seconds, which was remarkable in itself, and then when it was over the building, there was a tinkle of bells, and a rainbow fell out of Rudolph's arse, detached itself, and exploded, a multi-coloured firework that enveloped the police station wholly. Rudolph didn't stick around to see what happened next—his good deed for the day was done, apparently, and he fucked off into the distance without so much as a goodbye—but Finklefoot and Jimbo did, and it fairly impressed them both.

As the broken rainbow sherds tinkled down the building's exterior walls, all the possible entrances began to unlock. Windows clicked open, Fire Exit doors pulled

BABY RUDOLPH

outwards as if by the wind, and the main entrance, the one before which stood two very cold and drunken elves, undid its deadlock and eased itself open just an inch.

"Well," said Finklefoot. "I did not see that coming."

"Did you know he could do that?" Jimbo asked.

"Shitting rainbows?" said Finklefoot. "I had no idea. Thought he'd butt a door open for us with that big head of his. Magical turds were not on my bingo card for tonight."

"Bit of a cop-out, though, don't you think?" said Jimbo.

"Let's not talk about it," Finklefoot said, and he entered the station without even acknowledging the camera marked Fourth Wall to his left.

Once inside, which was marginally warmer than outside in the same way that Hell is slightly hotter than Texas, Finklefoot led Jimbo through the corridor (not plural, of course, since the LCPD station had been built on a budget and a whim) to where a steel door—apparently welded by Stevie Wonder on one of his off days—protruded from the wall. On the wall, about three quarters of the way up, there was an access control keypad.

"Well," said Jimbo. "That's just great. Shall I go and fetch Rudolph back? If we ask nicely, he might be able to spray some of his magic up the door."

"Ah, my dear Jimbo," Finklefoot said, tapping at his nose in that infuriating way people do when they're letting you know that they know something you don't. "I might be drunk, but I remember the code. I watched Quim put it in and memorised it."

Jimbo brightened a little. "Go on then," he said.

"I will," said Finklefoot, stalling momentarily. He *had* watched the Chief input the code yesterday, and he *had* memorised it, but that had been then, and now it was now, and he was drunk. "It was some of these numbers, combined to make a code," he said. "But which ones... what order... I..."

Jimbo kicked him in the shins. "Now is not the time to fall asleep again," he said. "Just put the code in so we can get this over with and I can go home. What is FF&J Investigations's policy on paid overtime, anyway?"

"It was 1234!" said Finklefoot. "Of course, because I remember thinking at the time, I thought, That's a fucking stupid code, anyone could get in!"

Jimbo tried it. It wasn't correct, and a red light told him so.

"Try 1111," Finklefoot said. "That sounds familiar."

Jimbo pushed the one button four times; a red light appeared once again on the panel. "Anything else sound familiar? Hey, what if this is one of those panels that, if you get it wrong three times, a bloody loud alarm goes off and the shutters all come down, trapping us in until the fuzz arrive to nick us?"

"Have you been watching *The Sweeney*?" Finklefoot said. "Try 999. That'll be it."

Tentatively, Jimbo keyed it in, and was so surprised when the keypad flashed a green light that he almost choked on his own tongue. There came a buzz, and then the door clicked, and Finklefoot pulled it open.

"See?" Finklefoot said, somehow managing to wink with both eyes at the same time. "I'm a genius."

It was colder than a witch's tit beneath the station; the corridor stretching all the way into the distance was slick with ice, and frozen stalactites hung down from the ceiling, threatening to snap off at any moment and impale anyone foolish enough to be walking below. Two such entities were just about to embark on the perilous journey from here to there when Jimbo said:

"Oooh, we could slide!"

Jimbo, shivering, said, "What?"

"Bit of a run-up, we can slide all the way down the corridor on the ice. Trust me, you don't want to walk it. I had the stitch yesterday; thought I was gonna pass out. Got my steps in, though."

Jimbo looked along the corridor, to where a column of light stretched out from the left right at the end. It did look a long way away, and he was already tired. "Okay, but we go together, on three."

"On three," said Finklefoot. "Try not to slip over, keep your core low to the ground."

"My core is *always* low to the ground," said Jimbo. "And the last time I checked, you weren't going to join the NBA any time soon, either."

And so, on the count of three, they kicked off the bottom step of the stairs they had just descended, and at something in the region of four-miles-per-hour—Usain Bolt, had he been aware of what was going on, would have been shitting himself—they slid along the corridor, and eventually arrived at the dimly-lit cell holding Krampus.

There was a grunt—up on the surface, those elves sleeping on top bunks were sent toppling to the floor, and a wedding party was interrupted as the yet-to-be-cut cake slipped to the right—as Krampus rolled over on his bed, opened his eyes, saw the two elves staring at him, and said, "Oh, fuck off, will you, I'm not interested."

BABY RUDOLPH

Jimbo took a step back. He was not being paid enough for this, if indeed he was being paid at all. They hadn't had the chance to finalise remuneration details on the walk over, but Finklefoot had kept using the term *pro bono, pro bono, pro bono,* my dear whateveryournameis, over and over, which Jimbo didn't think was a real word, so he hadn't pressed him further.

"I need— *we* need your help," Finklefoot said. "Last time, I promise."

"Yes, *pro bono*," added Jimbo, just because it seemed like a good place to use it. Also, he was terrified and couldn't put his words together correctly. Even in his head they were gobbledygook.

Krampus threw his huge goat legs over the edge of the bed and sat upright. "Anyone know what time it is?" he said.

They both looked at their watches and said, "Ten-past-nine," in unison.

"Sorry we're late," said Finklefoot. "It was Norm's fault."

"How can you be late?" Krampus said, rubbing sleep from his eyes. He rolled some of it up into a ball and flicked it at Jimbo. Luckily, there was a massive pane of two-inch-thick reinforced glass between them, and the eye-snot didn't make it through. "I didn't even know you were coming."

"It's annoying, I know, but as I explained to my friend here, if Norm had opened up at bang on Noon—"

"What the fuck do you want from me?" Krampus stood, took two unsteady steps toward the reinforced glass, and added, "So I can go back to bed. I was having a nice dream about butchering this entire race of elves, you see, and I want to see how it ended."

"!" Jimbo said.

"Now, now, Jimbo," said Finklefoot. "Sticks and stones break bones, but exclamation marks, well, they're just jolly rude." He took a step toward the glass, and then another, and a third, not that he was keeping count. "I need your assistance on the Ahora case," he said. "I have some new evidence I'd like to run by you."

At this, Krampus seemed amused. "Run by me," he said. "Run by—look, I'm only helping you because I've got nothing better to do with my time, not because I want this villain caught. As far as I'm concerned, good for them, glad they're up to no good, hope you *all* go missing eventually, but in the meantime, I'm fucking bored down here, so what do I get in return for my help this time?

Finklefoot pulled open the tray drawer, emptied his pockets into it, and slid it through to the other side.

BABY RUDOLPH

Krampus looked down at the contents of the drawer. "Hm, soggy bar snacks, my favourite." He emptied them into a plastic bowl, clingfilmed it, wrote the date on it with a marker pen, and put the bowl up on a shelf. Because if he'd learnt one thing in the past ten years, it was that keeping stock of your use-by-dates could be the difference between a mildly dodgy stomach and full-blown shits.

"This," said Finklefoot, holding the new piece of evidence up to the glass so that Krampus could examine it. "Found it in an alleyway next to a chloroformed handkerchief. Figured it was connected, somehow. Perhaps belonged to—"

"That's a Classic Cherry and Strawberry Carmex lip balm," said Krampus, and it was.

"Fucking hell!" said Finklefoot. "We weren't going to say it out loud."

"We were *saving* it," added Jimbo from behind. "For suspense purposes."

"Well, that's *that* idea fucked," said Finklefoot. "Yes, it's a Carmex lip balm of the strawberry and cherry variety," he went on with sheer annoyance, "and probably has something to do with the disappearance of one Ahora of the liquorice factory." He sighed, turned to give Jimbo a look that said,

Can you believe this guy? After all our ambiguity, he just comes out and says it. Prick.

"He wasn't to know, Eff-eff," Jimbo said. There was something about the huge, horned, half-goat, half-demon, all-bastard that made Jimbo want to say nice things about him. Strange that.

"I know, but still."

"Is this going to take all night?" Krampus asked, and he walked across to the side of the cell, grabbed a curtain with his talons, and began to walk it back. It was only when the curtain was half-drawn that Finklefoot said:

"Alright, alright, what do we do with this?" and he held the lip-balm out once again.

"I can think of at least one thing," Krampus said, "but, really, I'm sure you've already thought of the real answer, otherwise you wouldn't be wearing that monocle—" He pointed at Finklefoot, and then at Jimbo, "—or those pince-nez. You've started a detective agency, ain'tcha?" He waited a second, a grin forming about his thousand-fanged mouth. "Those are your gimmicks, aren't they? What, too good for an honest wheelchair or a bit of Alzheimer's, are you?"

"I actually considered a peg-leg, I'll have you know," said Finklefoot, "and Jimbo here is disabled at the best of times.

BABY RUDOLPH

Mocking the infirm now, are we, foul beast?" he said, bravely or stupidly, either way he was risking it.

Krampus nodded as if impressed; balls, it appeared, had been grown since their last encounter. Still made them low-hanging fruit, in Krampus's eyes, but there was definitely a look of admiration playing about his features. Either that or he was trying to clear some room in his stomach.

"How should we already know the answer to this new piece of evidence?" Jimbo said. He had to say something. The way these two were looking at each other, they were liable to fall in love.

If stating the obvious was an Olympic event, Krampus was about to stake his claim for Gold. "It's a lip-balm," he said.

"Yes," said Finklefoot. "It's a lip—bloody hell it's freezing down here, my pee-hole's frozen over—balm. A lip-balm. What are you suggesting? That we test it for lip prints?"

"Elves don't have lip prints," said Jimbo, only because he was feeling left out.

"I'm *suggesting*," said Krampus, teasing them with the curtain and removing another three feet of cell from their vision, "that you need someone who knows a lot about elf lips. Who's kissed a lot of elf lips. Who's sucked a lot of—"

"Jessica Claus!" Finklefoot said, beating Jimbo to it by a fraction of a second. The overall effect was like an echo, only underwater. And with elves.

"My, you *are* good detectives," teased Krampus. "That woman has kissed more lips than the Pope and Cassanova combined. It's a wonder your kind wasn't wiped out by herpes years ago. Take the lip-balm to Jessica Claus, and I'm sure she'll be able to tell you who wears that flavour."

"Genius!" Jimbo said.

"Thanks," Finklefoot replied. To Krampus he said, "Well, enjoy your damp pub snacks. There're some wasabi peanuts in there as well. Should warm you up a bit. Hate to think of you, freezing to death down here like this."

Krampus pulled the curtain the rest of the way across. "You get used to it," he said.

Jimbo and Finklefoot slowly headed for the stairs at the end of the corridor.

"That was really nice of him to help us like that," said Jimbo.

"Yeah, it was," Finklefoot replied, steadying himself on the wall. "Almost feel bad for being the one that put him down here in the first place."

BABY RUDOLPH

"And if I ever get out of here!" Krampus yelled out, "I'll rip the giblets out of both of you before you've even had a chance to piss yourself first!" Up on the surface, two cats started to fight for no reason, millions were lost as the Elfdaq100 fell to an all-time low, and the froth on Hattie Quim's cocoa sunk without a trace.

"I said 'almost', didn't I?"

"Yes, you did."

*

Rudolph's nightmare, you ask? The one awaiting him when he got home? If you must know, it was the one where he was mistaken for a non-magical reindeer by a short-sighted hunter, and spent the rest of his days—his mounted head did, at least—hanging on a wall, watching the short-sighted hunter's wife make venison sandwiches, that was, when she wasn't fornicating with the short-sighted hunter's brother, who had perfect twenty-twenty vision.

It was *that* nightmare.

18

The Paddock Arms was a magical reindeer-only venue, and so everything was the correct size and proportionate to that of its punters. Sure, reindeers could drink in any number of elf pubs, *The Partridge Inn* included—although they recommended booking first if your party was larger than three, as it left nowhere for the elves to sit—but who wanted to frequent places where you could easily accidentally step on a little fucker? You could never relax in a place like that, not really.

The Paddock Arms was near-empty when Rudolph arrived, and he didn't have trouble finding a table. When the waitress trotted over (although it was more of a canter than a trot, but that was only because of the heels she was wearing), Rudolph ordered a bottle of Malbec and two glasses.

"Expecting company?" the waitress said as she took away the food menu and wrapped cutlery.

"No, the extra glass is for when it comes back out," Rudolph said, which was a little rude, he thought, but ask stupid questions, expect a sarcastic, unwarranted answer.

BABY RUDOLPH

Off she cantered to deal with the drinks. *I shall apologise to her when she comes back*, Rudolph thought. *And compliment her on her heels. That ought to do it. They love being told they have pretty heels.*

He glanced about the place, which had undergone a bit of a refurbishment since he'd last been in. Mind you, that had been two-hundred years ago, when the fruit machine still had a massive crank on it and the Jackpot payout, adjusted for inflation, wouldn't buy a penny chew these days. Rudolph reminisced for a moment, lost in the black-and-white photos filling the main wall of the pub.

"Hang on a minute," Rudolph said, snapped suddenly from his lovely trot down Memory Lane by something that he should have noticed immediately after sitting down opposite the photo wall.

All the photos with him in them—seven in total, which had been hung in no particular order due to a former employee's apparent aversion to bar-work—had been scribbled on with black marker. Only his face was obscured with ink; the rest of the photos were visible. Seven thick black doodles where his head used to be. Rudolph was having none of it.

He summoned the waitress over, complimented her on her heels, and said, "What in fuckery has happened to my pictures?"

Although they had never met before, the waitress said, "Ah, I thought you might notice that, Mr. Dolph. I've tried everything: olive oil, Windex, vinegar, bleach, I can't get the bloody marker off. I don't know what ink she used, but it's tougher than a squirrel's nuts."

"Wait, are you telling me—did you just call me Mr. Dolph? No, never mind, one ridiculous thing at a time. You're telling me that some woman vandalised all the photos with me in them?"

The waitress nodded and pointed to the wall. "I've never seen her before, but she came in here yesterday and just went at them. I tried to confiscate the marker, but it was like trying to take a crayon from a very fat baby. You know how good their grip is. You've got more chance of winning the lottery."

"And that's all she did, is it?" Rudolph said, because you didn't have to be a rocket surgeon to work out who was responsible for this malicious act of vandalism. "Pink cardigan, big perm, funny accent?"

BABY RUDOLPH

"That's her," said the waitress. "Yeah, once she was done with the pictures, she called me a 'wee suitcase full of flanges' and did a runner."

Rudolph nodded and relaxed back in his chair; at some point during the exchange, he'd half-mounted the table. There was a massive hoof-mark where his food menu used to be.

As the waitress headed back to the bar, Rudolph tried to ingest what was happening, but it was like trying to swallow a television aerial... sideways, and without lube. When the waitress returned with a bottle of Malbec and two glasses, set them out on the table, Rudolph said, "You're not letting her back in here are you?" because now that he knew Merthyr was on the rampage, and also familiar with *The Paddock Arms*, he'd really rather have been somewhere else. *Anywhere* else.

"Forgive me for saying this," said the waitress, "because I'm not one to body-shame, or anything like that, but, and pardon me once again, but have you seen the fucking size of her? Do you know how little I get paid?" she went on. "I can tell you it's not worth losing my life over, so if she does come back, then I'm afraid you'll find me in the back, with the door locked."

"Thanks," Rudolph said, pouring himself a glass of red as the waitress went about her business again. He needed it now. Thankfully, he didn't have to drink alone for long, and soon, Wish was seated opposite him, listening to him talk with hooves beneath her chin and massive eyes glancing into his soul, as if there was something there that she liked, and was considering nicking it when he wasn't looking.

After several minutes of beating around the proverbial bush—"Did it take you long to fly here?" "Your hair looks amazing, and your heels are nice." "What, this nose? No, of course I don't polish it. It's naturally shiny."—Rudolph just came out with it.

"I think we have the same stalker," he said, chasing it down with a full glass of wine. He was already feeling a bit tipsy, but that's the thing with wine; if you're gonna make something from grapes, don't act surprised when people start necking it like juice.

"Nooooo," said Wish, smiling. "There are *hundreds* of stalkers out there. What are the odds of us having the exact same one?"

Maths had never been Rudolph's strong point, so he didn't do it. You can't be bad at something if you swerve it completely. "I've only known this woman for a few days," he said, visibly shivering, "but I've never been more scared of anything in my entire life. And I'm sure she makes you feel that way, too."

"How did you know mine was a 'she'?" Wish said, the smile instantly dropping from her face and being replaced by a wide, surprised maw. She looked like the back of a cross-channel ferry waiting for cars to get on board. "I never told anyone she was a 'she'."

"She is, though, isn't she? A she?"

"Yes," Wish admitted. "But that doesn't mean we have the same one. There are loads of shes out there. Probably an equal number of hes, and a growing number of theys. I'm a they, my stalker's a she, you're a he, your stalker's a she, so what? Nothing strange in that."

And there wasn't, as far as Rudolph was concerned, except for the fact that both he and Wish were in danger. "Does yours wear a pink cardigan?" he asked. "Big silly perm?"

"What is this, fucking *Guess Who*?" Wish said, laughing nervously. He'd struck a nerve, because Merthyr *was* their shared stalker, and that was both terrifying and yet comforting, because now Rudolph had someone to share with, and Wish could do likewise with him, and together they could somehow defeat her, like the final boss in a videogame. *Finish Her! Fatality.*

"Merthyr," they said simultaneously.

"Oh, I can't believe it!" said Wish, putting her glass down and refilling it.

"Nor can I," Rudolph said, shaking his head so hard that he gouged a hole in the wall with one of his antlers.

"Nor can I, ya wee cheating bastards, ya."

They both turned to face the door and the hulking brute of a potentially Scottish magical-reindeer-cum-psychopath standing between its frame. She was going for an off-the-shoulder, dragged-through-brambles-backwards, altogether scary as fuck look, and pulled it off with aplomb. Rudolph tried to move, but found out that his limbs had turned on him, and so he just sat there, glass of wine in one hoof with his mouth wide open. It must have been catching because Rudolph noticed Wish was doing the same. Like bad taxidermy, they were, put together by the short-sighted hunter of Rudolph's nightmares.

"So," said Merthyr, stepping into the pub proper, "this is whit's goan oan, ay? Whit's this, huh? Gang up oan Merthyr day, or hae yous two been up tae boggin' th'gither this hail time?"

BABY RUDOLPH

Rudolph didn't know what language this was now, but it was somehow the most terrifying, shit-your-pants, please don't hurt me, gooseflesh raising thing he had ever heard in his entire life. And she wasn't finished yet. As she stalked slowly across the room, which had fallen deafly silent apart from her heavy hoof-beats on bare floorboards, she continued.

"Ye 'n' Wish, huh?" she said, focussing entirely on Rudolph now, which wasn't, in his opinion, very fair at all. "Ye two-timing me, Rudy? Wi' yin o' mah offcasts?" To Wish she said, "Nae offence, darlin' bit ah stopped follaein ye months ago. Ye wur borin' me. Aye aff tae th' same places. Howfur mony bras does yin reindeer need, anyway?" She turned her intention back to Rudolph, who was trying to get his legs to work under the table, but so far had only succeeded in kicking a rat in the face.

"I think you should leave, Merthyr," Rudolph muttered, almost inaudibly. His tongue was about as useful as his legs, and both were about as useful as a motorcycle ashtray.

"Ah bet ye wid lik' that, wouldn't ye. Sae that ye 'n' wish 'ere kin gang hame 'n' mak' th' beast wi' two backs." She flicked her hair out of her face; her eyes were almost red now with either rage or reindeer pinkeye. "Ah teuk ye oan a crakin' day oot tae th' zoo. We hud a picnic in th' pairk, fur fuck's sake. We shot clay penguins th'gither. 'n' this is howfur ye repay me?"

"Look," said Rudolph, dry-swallowing. "I'm sorry, Merthyr, but I should have just told you then... fuck! I even tried to, but you wouldn't listen. We're never going to be more than friends. And I'm not sure we can even do that, now, and if I understood even half of what you were saying right now, I'd probably have a better idea of how to respond." He stopped, saw her face roll up into an angry scowl, and remained very still. Perhaps if he didn't move, she would leave him alone.

That's Tyrannosaurs, a tiny voice in his head told him.

"You have no right talking to anyone like that," said Wish to Merthyr, turning in her seat, her paralysis apparently broken. *Good for her*, Rudolph thought.

"Does he ken aboot yer fling wi' Blitzen? Hae ye tellt Rudy 'ere aboot howfur ye fucked Donner 'n' Dasher while Dancer gawked fae th' neuk o' th' stable?"

Wish looked down at the floor, seemingly embarrassed.

"Ah didnae think sae, ye wee munter. Sae dinnae stairt acting tough tae me. Ah will mak' ye keek aboot six inches tall."

BABY RUDOLPH

Rudolph had had enough. He just wanted to get out of there, out into the snow where it was big and there was plenty of room to fly away quickly.

The problem with that idyll, however, was Merthyr, who now stood directly between him and the exit, and didn't strike him as the sort of person who'd step aside if he asked nicely.

He got to his feet anyway. "Come on, Wish," he said. "We don't have to sit here and listen to this madness." Wish stood up; Rudolph could see she wanted to get out of there, too. Something about the way her legs bandied about beneath her, as if replaced by different-sized wooden pegs. Rudolph wanted to put a beermat under one of them to stop the wobble, but there was no time, and it would probably go off on its own eventually.

"Step aside, Merthyr," said Rudolph.

"Nae oan yer nelly," said Merthyr, which rang a bell somewhere in the dusty basement of Rudolph's mind, but with the dialect she used, he couldn't quite find it.

"Merthyr, I won't ask twice." He made himself as big as possible, which was still not big enough, but it was the thought that counted.

"Whit urr ye goan tae dae, Rudy?" she asked, and it was a damn good question. "A'll brain ye sae solid, yer legs wull turn intae accordians."

Nope.

None of that made any sense to him, so he took a step forward, and that was when three things happened all at once.

Firstly, the waitress ran into the back and locked the door. Later on, Officer Dufflecoat would question her about what had gone down, but since the only thing she'd seen had been the big sack of potatoes next to the telephone, her witness statement was brief and to the point: POTATOES, it said.

Secondly, the old man playing the fruit machine turned out three Lemons, and cash began to spill noisily into the tray. It was only the third time anyone had hit the Jackpot this century; pity that no one was paying attention, really.

And third and finally, Merthyr hit Rudolph so hard in the temple with a big, manicured hoof that he rolled across two tables, knocking menus and cutlery and uncollected glasses everywhere, and thumped into the jukebox, which of course switched itself on as a result and played *Kung Fu Fighting* by Carl Douglas for the rest of the scene.

BABY RUDOLPH

Rudolph was far too preoccupied with picking himself up to witness Wish's retribution, which was probably for the best as it didn't go the way it should have. Merthyr saw the right hook coming, ducked, swung around, and back-kicked Wish across the room like a bolting horse, annoyed at being whipped repeatedly by a jockey sick of coming fourth. Wish flew through the air, went past the geezer collecting his winnings from the fruit machine, and slammed into the photo wall. She was quickly buried beneath a heap of monochromatic memories from yesteryear.

Two caribou calves, sucking milkshakes through straws, watched the whole thing unfold with fascination while their mother took a shit in the next room. Officer Dufflecoat would question the mother later, on charges of neglect, but would quickly give up when the mother pulled out the "When Nature Calls" card, and he realised he was onto a loser.

"Ye pair o' bastards! Howfur dare ye dae this tae me!"

Like a reindeer scorned, Merthyr bounded across the room. Below the surface, Krampus rolled out of his bunk, curled up into the foetal position on the ice-cold floor, and called out plaintively for his mommy.

Back to his hooves, Rudolph steeled himself for impact. The music continued to pour from the jukebox speakers, and Rudolph had just enough time to think, *Not everybody could have been Kung Fu fighting. Surely.*

"Let's see howfur bricht yer hooter shines efter this yin!" said Merthyr, and she, against all laws of physics known to man, but apparently not to magical reindeer, launched herself into the air, turned around twice, and caught Rudolph in the chops with a trailing leg.

Quite annoyed at being almost knocked out for a second time, Rudolph rolled across the sawdust floor and came to rest against the hind legs of the elderly reindeer who'd just finished filling a tatty, hessian sack with his winnings.

"Here," said the elder, dropping the bag of coins at Rudolph's hooves. "And don't say us elderly have no place in society and should be euthanised at fifteen-hundred."

Rudolph got unsteadily back to his feet and snatched up the sack of coins. "Thanks, old-timer," he said. "But there are some things I refuse to budge from, and any reindeer that shits itself at will and spends its days at home watching *Antiques Roadshow* and shouting at calves playing on its lawn, well, off to Switzerland you should go." He sucked in a huge lungful of air. "Just my opinion, of course."

BABY RUDOLPH

"Like assholes," the elder said, "we all have one."

"Look out!" Wish cried from across the room, where she was frantically trying to remove a picture frame from around her left antler.

Rudolph turned round, saw Merthyr coming toward him, and started to swing the sack of coins, round and round and round.

The old pool-balls-in-a-sock trick. You didn't see much of that nowadays, but way back when, you couldn't walk into a bar without getting clipped by a carefully-crafted two reds and a yellow in a Christmas stocking. By the time you reached the bar, you'd been hit so many times you didn't need a drink to feel all fuzzy and suffer a headache the next day, so you'd just leave without ordering anything. Saved a fortune on a night out.

"Aff tae skelp me wi' that, urr ye? That'll gang doon weel wi' a' yer wee fans, wilnae it, babeh Rudy?"

"I DON'T KNOW WHAT YOU ARE SAYING!" Rudolph screamed back. It was like trying to understand a baby who'd found the key to the liquor cabinet; he'd had conversations with flies that had made more sense.

Swoop, swoop, swoop went the coin sack, and then, as Rudolph took two steps forwards, the bag went *chink-thunk!* as it came into contact with Merthyr's cheek.

The pair of milkshake-sucking calves stopped sucking, momentarily. They hadn't seen anything like this since their parents' "trial separation".

For a moment, nothing seemed to happen. The coin sack in Rudolph's clenched hoof (don't ask) just dangled next to Merthyr's head, swinging slowly back and forth. Merthyr's eyes were wider now than ever before, and when she spoke, it was clear that a mistake had been made, but not to worry, mistakes can be rectified.

A couple of rainbow droppings fell out of Rudolph; *The Paddock Inn* would, later that year, win the inaugural *Bar of the Year Award*, and some would say it was those droppings that had done it. But that was not important right now.

"Did ye juist whallop me wi' a poke o' coins?" Merthyr said, spitting out what appeared to be a molar. The tooth hit Rudolph directly between the eyes and then proceeded to rattle across the floorboards for so long that it became a Dubstep hit. "Ye shouldn't hae dane that, babeh rudy. A've bin keekin efter mah wee teeth sin ah wis a bairn, 'n' ye'v gaen

BABY RUDOLPH

'n' knocked yin oot." As an afterthought, she added, "Ya wee prick!"

"Sorry?" Rudolph squeaked, lowering the sack of coins.

"You shouldn't have done that, son," said the elder from somewhere behind. "Hitting her was all well and good, but you don't go messing around with someone's teeth. What's the *matter* with you, man?"

Merthyr took a slow, steady step back and somehow managed to get a whole hoof into her mouth, feeling around for the missing tooth. Rudolph could have saved her some time; it was on the floor, still rattling about, apparently working on a second verse.

"A'm goan tae tear ye limb fae limb—"

That was as far as Merthyr got before Wish slammed into the side of her, carrying them both through the air and crashing into the abandoned bar. Refurbishments were all well and good, but not when you had to *keep* making them. You didn't get this sort of damage in an elf establishment. When a fight broke out in an elf pub, you might find yourself picking up a toppled chair or two, and if it was a *really* bad brawl, re-hang the dartboard and order some new pool cues.

The mother who would later be arrested, questioned, and released on jumped-up neglect charges emerged from the

Ladies' room, saw the mess all around the bar, and said, "This place has really gone downhill," before taking a seat with her calves and continuing with her fungi-burger.

Wish had mounted Merthyr now and was, if you are familiar with the UFC, unleashing a torrent of ground and pound, but Merthyr was strong, and fairly quick. All it took was one buck (which is what *all* female deer say when they find themselves suddenly with child) and Merthyr was out from under Wish and getting back to her hooves.

This is getting ridiculous now, Rudolph thought. But not for the fruit machine-playing elder, who had set up a bookies across the room and was taking bets from several gambling elders.

"Ahm nae playin' aroond any mair, ya wee hoor!" Merthyr said, wiping blood from her nose and flicking it across the room, where it began to sizzle and smoke, before burning through the floorboard entirely and dropping down into the cellar below. The sudden threat of fire was immediately dismissed as the blood landed in an open barrel of non-flammable beer and went out with one final hiss.

Close, though.

BABY RUDOLPH

"Just leave Rudolph alone!" Wish said. "He's not interested in you, and only went out with you because he felt sorry for you."

Rudolph balked at this. That wasn't the reason, was it? Sure, it played a part, but it wasn't the *only* reason. He'd defended Merthyr in the practise stables, the same way she'd defended him at the Secret Comedy Club. They were, if nothing else, simpatico, two sides of the same coin, and both no stranger to bullying.

"That's enough," Rudolph said, limping slowly across the room. "No more fighting."

Over in the corner, the gambling (not gambolling, that would put a different spin on things entirely) elders collectively moaned and began to demand their money back from the centuries' old fruit machine player.

"But she's *stalking* you, Rudolph," said Wish. "Just like she stalked me, and Santa *knows* how many before us!"

Rudolph waved these claims away with a tired, most probably broken, front leg. At least he no longer needed an excuse not to train. That leg was *definitely* fucked up.

"Merthyr," Rudolph said. "I apologise."

Her face softened; the blood dripping from the end of her nose came to a complete halt, as if someone had hit pause on the whole thing. They were close enough now for their antlers to intertwine, which they did. Speaking of which, most antlered beasts use them as weapons during scuffles with rivals, but these are anthropomorphic magical reindeer we're talking about here, so normal rules didn't apply. Also, it wouldn't have been half as much fun if they'd just rattled back and forth like they invariably do on Earth. You might as well watch paint dry.

"I apologise for leading you on, and I'm sorry that it's come to this." Rudolph extended his floppy leg, and she looked at it, eyes glistening with tears yet to come. "I'm sorry—"

Merthyr clobbered him to the temple, but not before giving his gammy leg a full twist first, and as she flew toward the exit, leaving carnage in her wake, she said, "Ahm no acceptin' ony apologies, ya wee jobby! Ahm goan tae follow ye 'til th' day ye die!"

As if to punctuate her departure, the final black-and-white picture—which had been clinging on for dear life, looking down at the fallen and praying to the Gods not to take him, too—fell from the wall.

BABY RUDOLPH

Rudolph picked himself up yet again, apologised to the floorboards ("We really must stop meeting like this!") and turned to face Wish, who was looking mightily despondent.

"What was all that about?" she said. "That's not how to deal with psychos like her, Rudolph. She'll only be worse from here on in. Don't be surprised to wake up tomorrow morning next to a seal head."

"I know, but what else could I say? She obviously needs help, and—"

"Does she come across as the type of deer who's going to make an appointment any time soon?"

Rudolph had to admit that Wish had a point, and so did he, apparently.

"And calm yourself down," said Wish, "your lipstick's been out for the past five minutes, and I didn't want to say anything just in case it was just adrenaline."

Rudolph looked down and through his legs. Wish was right. He sucked his lipstick in and came back up to find that Wish was already cantering, not trotting, definitely not sauntering, toward the exit. As she passed the rudimentary bookies, she tossed a coin at the elder fruity-player and said, "Fifty pence says he's dead before Christmas."

Rudolph slumped to the ground, heart still racing in his chest, and huffed depressingly through both nostrils.

Five minutes later there was an audible click, the sound of very nice heels on wood, and then a trepidatious voice said, "Is she gone, Mr. Dolph?"

Merthyr? Was she gone?

"From *here*, yes," Rudolph said, spitting out blood that didn't singe the floorboards but left a really nasty stain.

"From *me*, I doubt it."

BABY RUDOLPH

19

"Krampus told you what?"

Finklefoot was growing tired of repeating himself. At this point, he was considering putting the whole thing out as an audiobook so that she could listen to it at her pleasure.

"No one knows more about the lips of elfish men than you," said Finklefoot for the umpteenth time. Jessica Clause had never struck him as a genius, but he'd never had her down as a total *Love Island* reject, either. Shows how your impressions can be skewed when you've got a faceful of cleavage to contend with.

"So, what's this got to do with *me* again?" she said, also for the umpteenth time. It would, Finklefoot thought, probably sink in more if she weren't upside down on a pole with her legs apart. And just what was that smell any—

"Your husband," Jimbo said. "Father Christmas, aka Saint Nick, aka The Fat Bastard, aka—"

"Swollen Red Suit!" she interrupted. "Oh, I do like this game!"

"Yes, quite," said Finklefoot, readjusting his monocle so that he could only see one of her again. "Well, look, Mrs Claus, I know you're busy rehearsing, and that's great—"

"Oh, you are taking part as well, aren't you?" she said, flinging herself up and around and about and then down again. It was like watching a squirrel with its head caught in a birdfeeder. A squirrel with massive tits. "It's going to be so much fun!"

"Actually, we're a *Bee Gees* tribute act," said Jimbo, adjusting his pince-nez so that he could see *more* of her. Unlike his friend, he rather liked the way human women were put together.

"We are not a *Bee Gees* tribu—"

"I love the *Bee Gees*!" said Jessica Claus as she dismounted. "Please tell me you'll sing 'Massachusetts'." She began dragging a towel all over the damp bits of her body, paying particular attention to her—

"*Sing* it?" Finklefoot said. "On the best of days, you'll find we can't even *say* it." It was true, and to prove it he said, "Machas... Machu Pichu... Masochistic... see?"

"I *do* see," said Jessica Claus, dropping the wet towel on top of Finklefoot's head. "So, what was it you wanted help with again?"

BABY RUDOLPH

There is a common urban legend, told by grandelves to their grandelflings for no other reason than to stop them from doing it, that if you roll your eyes too many times in one day, you'll wake up the next morning staring at the back of your own head... from the inside. Whether this was true remained to be seen, but Finklefoot was pushing his luck, either way.

"This lip-balm," he said, holding it up. "We believe that whoever this belongs to elfnapped Ahora and is currently holding her somewhere."

"Or has killed her and she'll turn up dead eventually," added Jimbo.

"Yes, well, that is also a theory, but let's not kill our chickens before they don't hatch, as it were." Finklefoot took the towel from his head and chucked it into a corner. "Elf lips," he continued, "are a specialty of yours, and you might be able to help us—"

"You think I can tell you who that belongs to just by looking at it?" she said, pointing at the lip-balm.

"No, but the flavour," said Finklefoot. "The flavour is a dead giveaway, isn't it?"

"Put it on and kiss me."

Something happened then, in that moment, which had probably never happened before in the history of elfkind, or at least since recorded history began, which was still ages ago. And that was this: Finklefoot, who had been holding the lip-balm out with one hand for Jessica Clause to see, lost consciousness. Behind him, still trying to fathom why women's breasts looked better than elf breasts—something to do with nipple placement, he'd surmised—also passed out. Their trajectories, the directions they were falling in, meant that their heads came together with a mighty thud!, which brought them back to their feet and subsequently consciousness, albeit with jaws still hanging agog as if they'd just been told they'd won the lottery, but unfortunately wouldn't have time to spend it because of an errant asteroid.

"I'm sorry," said Finklefoot, rubbing at his head, which hurt and he had no idea why. "Something came over me."

"Mmm," said Jessica Claus. "I know that feeling."

"Did you ask me to put this lip-balm on and kiss you?" He felt himself going dizzy again; he wished she'd put some fucking clothes on.

"It's the only way I'll know who wears it," she said.

"Couldn't you just give it a sniff," Jimbo said. "Or put it on the back of your hand and kiss that?" He was jealous she hadn't asked *him* to kiss her, and it would look a little needy if he offered himself up. *You have a wife at home,* an afterthought reminded him. *A beautiful wife whose nipples might look like crossed eyes, but she makes a lovely sandwich...*

"I *could*," Jessica Claus said. "But I don't want to."

Finklefoot sighed; the things he did for his country.

"I'll do it," he said. "But I'm only doing it for Ahora. If this gets back to my wife, she'll not only have my guts for garters, she'll also have my skin for lampshades, my skull for an ashtray, and my bollocks for earrings." He uncapped the lip-balm and began to apply it to his lips.

Jessica Claus smiled as she watched.

Jammy prick! Jimbo thought, already making plans to accidentally let slip the next time he saw Trixie.

"That's a good little fella," said Jessica. She was pinching her own nipples as she watched. What that was all about, Jimbo didn't know. His wife *never* pinched hers; she only used them to keep her knitting untangled.

"Okay!" Finklefoot said, satisfied he'd given his lips a generous coat. In truth, most of it was on his beard. "Let's get this over with."

Jessica Claus dropped into a crouch; something squeaked beneath her, like a balloon being slowly let down, but neither Finklefoot nor Jimbo wanted to ask.

She pulled Finklefoot closer, licked her own lips, and then they kissed. It wasn't erotic at all, so put the tissues away. Jimbo had seen more passionate barnacles. It was like watching your uncle kiss your aunt. Nothing to wank home about. When it was over—and not a moment too soon, as far as Jimbo was concerned—both parties looked confused, as well they should. Jessica Claus stood up, with further mysterious squeakings, and looked down at Finklefoot with disgust.

"You really *do* love your wife, don't you?" she said.

"With every ounce of me," he replied, rubbing the residue from his lips and beard.

"I love mine more," said Jimbo, "obviously, because I would *never* have kissed you."

"Who? Me?" said Finklefoot, confused.

"No," replied Jimbo. "*Her* there with the... the shiny tits and the tinsel bush..."

Finklefoot shook his head and turned back to Jessica Claus, who appeared to still be thinking. She ran her tongue over her top lip, and then the bottom, all the time frowning.

BABY RUDOLPH

"Well?" Finklefoot urged.

After about a minute of further considerations, she said, "It rings a bell." She puckered her lips, licked them again. "I've definitely kissed the wearer of that lip-balm before, that much I know is true, but... it's on the tip of my tongue."

"That might just be a bit of beard," said Jimbo.

"Shush, dickhead," said Finklefoot to his friend. "Can't you see she's thinking? This could be it. We can nail this sonofabitch, find Ahora, dead or alive, and get back to the factory in time for tomorrow."

"We've got songs to practice," Jimbo reminded him.

"We are not a fucking *Bee Gees* tribu—"

"Nope!" Jessica Claus said, interrupting the elves before the argument had had a chance to really get going.

"Nope?" said Finklefoot.

"Nope?" echoed Jimbo.

"Uh-huh. Nope," said Jessica Claus.

"Nope as in...?" Finklefoot said.

"As in I definitely exchanged fluids with someone, and that someone had been wearing Classic Cherry and Strawberry Carmex at the time, but for the life of me, I can't recall who it was, which is odd because at the time I thought it had been strange. I mean, what kind of elf wears flavoured lip-balm when he's going down—"

"So that's it, is it?" sighed Finklefoot. "We're back to square one."

"I'm tired," Jimbo said. "Can we go to the pub yet?"

"I'm sorry I couldn't help you, but you'll be the first to know if it comes back to me." She finally pulled on a dressing gown and tied it at the waist. She could have done that five minutes ago, but where was the fun in that? She liked it when she walked into a room to meet elves, only to exit the same room, leaving behind bearded tripods. "I'll let The Fat Bastard know that you're doing your utmost, but probably best to keep our little kiss a secret. He can get awfully jealous if his castle is breached, so to speak." And with that, she left and closed the practice room door behind her, leaving Finklefoot and Jimbo dejected once again.

"Worst kiss ever," said Jimbo.

"Are there any walk-in clinics open this time of day?" asked Finklefoot. "I'm going to need some tests doing, pronto."

*

BABY RUDOLPH

The flight home from the pub gave Rudolph plenty of time to think about what had just happened. The date (non-date?) with Wish, the arrival of Merthyr, the ensuing brawl, the police interrogation, all of it weighed so heavily on Rudolph's mind that it was all he could do to stay airborne.

How had life turned on him so brutally? This time last week everything was ordinary. Days of training, leading to nights of blissful nothingness, five days a week, with pointless trots around town at the weekend. So normal. So boring. And yet, as Rudolph overtook a murmuration of starlings, how he yearned to go back.

Simpler times.

"The fuck do you think you're playing at?"

Rudolph turned his head to find a starling had landed on his shoulder, and was now looking at him intensely, with severe scrutiny, as if Rudolph had just plucked all the feathers from its bastard-wing to make little quills out of, like the ones they use in Paddy Power.

"Sorry?" replied Rudolph.

"I said, what in the name of fuckery do you think you're playing at?" repeated the bird. "We're up here making pretty patterns in the sky, and you just plough through us as if we aren't even there. You mad, or something?"

Rudolph shook his head. "I'm terribly sorry," he said. "Just got a lot on my mind at the—"

"I don't care if your mother's just been shot by hunters and you're wondering if the life-insurance'll cover the funeral," said the starling. "You don't just interrupt us mid-flow like that. Could have killed a hundred of us, you prick."

Why does everyone keep yelling at me? Rudolph thought, feeling sorry for himself.

"I'm truly sorry," he said. "I'll be more careful next time."

"Better not be a next time," said the little bird. "I'll fuck you up." And then it flew away, its tiny wings flapping so rapidly that Rudolph couldn't even see them.

He sighed, and dropped a thousand feet, preparatory to landing. He just wanted his bedding now. Lock the stable door and leave the entire world outside. *Don't even switch the computer on*, he told himself, knowing that there would be a barrage of angry, misspelt messages awaiting him from She Who Stalks Behind the Rows. He couldn't face such derangement; it was liable to push him over the edge, and he'd end up back at the pub, drowning his sorrows.

He steered himself right and dropped down to rooftop level. He saw the roof of his stable up ahead. Safety. Silence. Solace. He was mid-sigh with relief when he saw her, and suddenly, his brain told him it would never end, that it was best to just stretch himself out, become a kamikaze missile, and hit the ground as hard as he could head-first.

Merthyr was in front of his stable. Just sitting there on the kerb, forelegs crossed and hind legs spread out behind her. Positioned so that she would see him arrive, see him leave, and unless he drew his curtains, see everything he was doing inside.

Pulling a sharp left—in the nick of time, too, as Merthyr looked up to the sky, anticipating his return—Rudolph came in to land three streets away and touched down in the thick snow with all the grace of a heron whose head had fallen off, as they invariably do when they come into contact with buckshot from the shotgun of a farmer whose dwindling Koi collection had to be protected at all costs.

"Fuck!" said Rudolph.

"Potty-mouth," a passing elf said.

Well, that's just grand, that is, thought Rudolph. *I can't even go home. I'm homeless! I'm a hobo!* "Can I have some spare change please?" he called after the departing elf, because there was no time like the present to start honing up those begging skills.

And so it came to be, Rudolph was finally brought to his knees by Merthyr Titful. That stark-raving, binge-eating, delusional, big-permed, cardigan-wearing, bloated sack of craziness who had seemed so nice to him at one point before turning into a terror in reindeer form. That absolute cunt!

Rudolph sobbed, dragged himself across the street, and fell asleep next to an industrial bin outside a hairdresser's shop.

This time, the nightmares were *all* about Merthyr.

20

The day of the Land of Christmas Annual Variety Show arrived so quickly, one could be forgiven for thinking certain bits had been missed out. Important bits, perhaps, that would have taken up at least another twenty pages, and made the whole thing run more smoothly. In fact, that was not the case at all. Between Rudolph collapsing in tears—three streets from what was once his sanctuary—to the morning of the big event, nothing at all happened, and no one wants to read about that.

Town Hall was a-bustle with activity, as things were carried in and the same things were carried out again, because someone had forgotten to arrange the chairs into neat, symmetrical rows first. Speakers were plugged in, tested, equalised, tested again, and the finishing touches were made to backdrops and props. The smell of still-tacky paint hung in the atmosphere like farts in lifts. Backstage, performers went through their scales, their dance moves, and in one case, an entire cutlery drawer. You couldn't move for singers, dancers, and comedians. Whoever had given the school dance troupe the go-ahead, though, had a lot to answer for.

Those little fuckers were everywhere, all dressed up like swans and ninjas; it was a logistical nightmare.

Finklefoot and Jimbo arrived on the scene—and what a scene it was, too!—took one look at it, and decided the pub was a better option. Rat had pre-empted the Town Hall chaos, skipped it entirely, and was already in his place at the bar when they arrived.

"So," said Norm, pushing their pints of 'the usual' across the sticky bar-top. "What slot did you get?"

"Three pm," whined Finklefoot. "And I wouldn't be doing it if *someone*—" he gave Jimbo a filthy look, the kind that could melt ice-cubes or clear soft-play areas, "—is a blackmailing bastard."

Jimbo rolled his eyes.

"Shouldn't do that," said Rat, blowing the froth from his pint. "My grandpa once told me he knew someone who rolled his eyes so much, one day he woke up and he could read the tag on the neck of his shirt."

"Bollocks!" said Jimbo, and so that was the end of that barnstorming conversation.

"I'm on after Shart's knife and fork blood-fest," Norm said, drawing a large Scotch from the optic. "I hope they mop the stage properly, otherwise there'll be arrows everywhere."

BABY RUDOLPH

"Arrows?" said Rat. "What's that all about then?"

"You had to be there," said Finklefoot, grimly, "but turns out our landlord here is a direct descendant of Robin Hood." He mimed archery, which is the quickest way of describing the nonsense he was doing with his hands.

"Bloody good at it, too," Jimbo said. "If ever war breaks out, I know who I'm standing behind with my eyes closed."

"I just find all this... this *celebration* to be in bad taste," Finklefoot said. "I mean, Ahora of the jigsaw factory is still missing, and no one's any the wiser as to what happened to her, or who could have elfnapped her." He sank half his pint in one go, lit his pipe, and slumped into a sulk.

"Fucking Debbie Downer," said Rat, which was more than a little insensitive, but that was Rat for you. When his grandpa died, the one who told him the nonsense about eye-rolling, Rat had organised a DJ for the funeral. *It's what he would have wanted*, he'd told the distraught attendees as they'd quickly filed out of the church, covered in poppers and trying to remove luminous wristbands and chokers from their persons. In other words, Rat had less tact than he had kidneys.

"If Jessica Claus could just *remember*," said Finklefoot, blowing thick, blue smoke into the room. "If she wasn't such a slut for us little people..." He tailed off there, knowing he was about to get himself into trouble, and quite right, too.

They spent the next hour drinking in silence. The *Bee Gees* and Legolas the Fifteenth.

It was going to be an awfully long day, indeed.

*

"Ladies and gentlemen, elves and elflings, magical talking anthropomorphs from all four corners of the land, please put your hands, hooves, and paws together for this, our Land of Christmas Annual Variety Show!"

Applause filled Town Hall, which hadn't heard such a racket since the last time Tyler Swaft performed there. Not a dry seat in the house that night, for Tyler Swaft was to housewives what AR15s are to Alabama. Once the trigger's pulled, it's hard to stop the squirt. As mixed metaphors go, that one's the bee's bollocks.

Dorman moved across the stage, microphone cord trailing behind him like a steroid-using rat's tail. Or do rat's tails shrink when roids are involved? Jury was out on that one, but you get the idea.

BABY RUDOLPH

"Boy, do we have a show for you today, folks," he said, fiddling with his bow-tie. "We've got dancers, singers, magicians, stand-up comics, escapologists, and choirs." *God, it's warm up here*, he thought, unbuttoning his top button. He loved being a compère, would rather be doing nothing else, but it didn't half play havoc with his laundry schedule. Not to mention his downstairs arrangement.

The crowd seemed to not notice, however. They just clapped and cheered and hollered like any good audience should. Except at an execution by lethal injection, perhaps.

"First out today, we have The Brothers Blimp and their incredible mime act!"

"Oh," said the audience, collectively. One elf said, "Pissing mime," as if he'd had bad experiences with it in the past, and the mere mention of it triggered his sensibilities.

*

"Jessica!"

Finklefoot rushed after her as she sauntered through the corridors, half-dressed (or half-undressed, depending on which way you saw things) and with an elf-slave flanking her on either side. She was walking them! Walking them like dogs! And they were wearing spiky, leather collars, too, but not much else. Who did she think she was? Madonna? When she heard Finklefoot calling her name, she stopped, turned slowly around, and smiled seductively. One of the elf-slaves, still on all-fours, took a piss up the wall.

"Jessica," panted Finklefoot. "Any more thoughts about..." He looked at the elf-slaves either side of her and lowered his voice. "About you know what?" he whispered from the corner of his mouth.

"Oh, yeah!" she said, which raised Finklefoot's hopes somewhat. "Nope," she said, which dropped them again and crushed them under her marvellous heels! "Well, sort of," she continued, which was neither here nor there in the grand scheme of things, but it was better than a straight no. "I was lying in bed last night, and He was snoring next to me, because his CPAP machine's on the blink and he's too cheap to get a new one." She paused, which gave Finklefoot just enough time to regret his decision to engage her at all. "Well," she went on, "I thought I had it, something about handcuffs for a minute, and then the more I thought about it, the foggier it all got, so I just went to sleep instead."

Well, thought Finklefoot. *That was quite a story, and might do well if she self-published it, but it was never going to sell enough copies for her to become the voice of treason on Twatter.*

"Handcuffs?" he said.

"Not right now, darling," she replied. "I've got time for one more practice and these little bastards ain't going to walk themselves."

She turned, she walked, she disappeared amongst the rabble.

"Why's it gone so damn quiet out there?" Finklefoot asked anyone near enough to hear.

"Mimes," said a little elfling dressed as a swan. Cute, she was. Like butter wouldn't melt. "*No one* likes fucking mimes," she said, and spat on the floor.

*

After The Brothers Blimp were chased off with rotten fruit—remaining in character, of course, they pretended the flying tomatoes were a swarm of wasps, which got them their only laugh of their routine—it was Officer Dufflecoat and Detective Quim's turn on stage, and they whipped the audience up into a frenzy with their Cops & Robbers dance number to the *Benny Hill* theme tune. It wasn't terrible, but they lost the younger audience members when the background dancers came out, all dressed as Jimmy Savile, but won them back again when the truncheons started to swing and silver wigs and cigars started flying hither and thither.

Next up was Callie Broccoli, whose own brand of ultra-feminist comedy fell on deaf ears, and those that could still hear proceeded to punch their own eardrums until they couldn't.

"Thank Santa!" someone cried out when Shart took to the stage next. This came as a shock to Shart, who hadn't realised he had any fans. It made sense then when he scanned the audience and saw his mother with a megaphone and a sign that said, "Not too deep, son! We don't have insurance!"

Several gallons of blood were unleashed onto the stage in the next fifteen minutes, as Shart worked his way through forks, knives, spoons, screwdrivers, corkscrews and chopsticks. His big finale, involving two coat-hangers and a trapeze bar, divided the audience so much that a fight broke out. A national newspaper would later go on to say, *Though not for the faint of heart, Shart brought blood, guts, and some poo to an otherwise mediocre afternoon. Also, three foxes and two elves have now been identified, and are currently under investigation for the parts they played in the ensuing melee.*

*

"This is ridiculous," Finklefoot said, adjusting his wig. "I mean look at us! You two look like drunken Beatles, and I look like Roy Orbison's older, shorter brother."

"I think we look all right," said Jimbo, admiring himself in the mirror. "Just try not to think about what you look like," he continued. "It's all about the singing. Our voices."

"Oh yes!" said Finklefoot, haughtily. "Our voices. Do we kick each other in the bollocks now or wait until we get on stage?"

"We're *elves*," Rat said, trying to flatten one side of his huge collar. "Our voices are *already* high-pitched. Naturally. All we've got to do is work through the medley, try not to trip over the microphone cord, look sexy for the housewives, and the rest will take care of itself."

Finklefoot did not share the optimism of his bandmate. It would be a miracle if they weren't back here in half an hour, dripping with veg and wondering at what point it went wrong. And 'look sexy for the housewives'? How in the name of fuckery were they going to pull that one off, dressed like this, with syrups like these on their heads? Tyler Swaft they most definitely were not.

Deep breaths, it'll all be over soon.

*

Rudolph sat in his dressing-room, looking at his reflection and powdering his antlers. "This comedian retires today," he said. The voice in his head said, *It'll all be over soon.*

*

Ahora of the jigsaw factory listened to the faint sound of music, of cheers, of applause, of merriment. She was on her second rat of the day, and this one was bitter, but she had to eat *something*. She was only glad that her captor, that maniac, hadn't been to empty her ablutions, or tell her for the hundredth time that everything was fine, she was safe, and it'll all be over soon.

*

BABY RUDOLPH

Jessica Claus slapped one of her elf-slaves across the face with a soggy mackerel, kissed him on the nose and laughed. "Don't worry, you sexy, little bastards," she said, kicking the second elf-slave square in the chestnuts. "It'll all be over soon."

*

At the Town Hall's double-doors, Merthyr huffed, handed the bouncers a fiver, and waited for them to step aside before entering. She grinned, did the Kubrick stare for no real reason and to no one in particular, and calmly said:

"It'll all be over soon, ya wee bunch o' bastards."

21

The audience watched expectantly as Norm, who had served many of them beers and spirits and cocktails, faced down the target across the stage. For a moment there was complete silence as all eyes fell upon Norm, then the three balloons, Norm, then the three balloons. They watched as Norm assumed a shooting position and nocked an arrow, then drew and anchored the bow, and took deep, steady breaths as he took aim.

It was all academic, really, because Norm hadn't missed in years. He was simply stringing the crowd along. No one likes a cocky cunt.

He breathed in and released the string.

The first balloon—a red one, not that it really mattered—popped and suddenly wasn't there anymore, which is what happens to all good balloons when they die. Its corpse hung limply beneath the arrowhead like a condom about to be flushed.

The audience went wild, but were soon urging each other to settle down, he has two more to go, the first one could have been a fluke. He was just a barman, after all. How good could he really be?

Norm exploded the two remaining balloons with about as much effort as it takes a wasp to go *bzzz*. No one in the room could believe what they had just seen, but they *had* seen it, hadn't they?

"I'll never try to worm my way out of paying my tab again," said one elf to his neighbour.

"That's a bloody good point!" his neighbour replied, suddenly panicking and riffling through his pockets. "I still owe him for that buffet he put on for our Sharon's birthday do."

Norm took his bow and headed for the wings, satisfied with his performance, although the last one splitting the first arrow and still popping the third balloon anyway had made his heart jump into his throat, but all-in-all he was happy that the arrows had mostly done what he'd told them to.

"Wow!" Dorman said, veritably dancing onto the stage. "Wasn't that something?" He'd abandoned the wearing of a bowtie completely now; it just wasn't feasible, given the atmosphere. "Right, who's ready for our next act?" he went on as the stage was cleared and prepared for things to come.

A three-tier set of wooden bleachers was wheeled out behind him, so it was obvious what was up next.

"Fucking choirs!" one elf called out.

"Just a bunch of wankers!" said a second.

A couple of mutters and boos came in response, but the consensus was that the two disgruntled elves were not lying.

"In honour of Ahora, who will be sorely missed, even though she hasn't turned up dead yet, Hattie Quim took over the jigsaw factory choir when they had no one else to turn to. At short notice, she's been collaborating with them to bring you an all-new composition. Fabulous beings of the Land of Christmas, please give a warm welcome to the Jigsaw Factory Choir, performing 'If It Wasn't for Hattie, We Wouldn't Be Here.'"

Dorman vacated the stage, but he had to fight his way through twenty onrushing geriatrics doing vocal warm-up exercises first. The smell of Cherry Bakewells and urine was enough to make him gag.

Once assembled—which took about as long as an Ikea wardrobe—the choir stood silent and still, awaiting their saviour.

Hattie Quim had never been shy. And not just when it came to pissing in alleyways. She was an attention-seeker of the highest order, the kind of conceited bitch that would throw you under a bus, literally, if it meant she went viral. Her husband, the Chief of police, of course defended her character unequivocally, but usually under threat of a sex-ban.

It was no surprise then when she took to the stage in full royal regalia. The crown balanced atop her silver beehive had been borrowed—term used very loosely, as they were pretty pissed off about it, and still hadn't figured out where it could have got to—from Earth's *Victoria and Albert Museum*, and the dress was from the M*useo del Traje* in Madrid, because everyone knows you don't nick from the same place twice. Both were, of course, far too big for her, but that didn't stop Hattie Quim. She was nothing if not a tryer. Very trying, she was.

"Fucking choir!" said the vocal elf, newly enraged and jumping to his feet. When he saw he was on his own, he sat back down. "Fucking choir," he whispered.

The choir began to sing, and it was—

*

"A load of bollocks," Ahora said, giving the bars of her cell a good kick. The music was so close, it owed her an apology for invading her space. "What a racket! What's she done to my choir? They never used to make that noise. She's broken them. She's broken the choir!" She stuffed a dead rat in each ear. "I shouldn't have to listen to that! What is this? Some kind of sick torture? HELP! HELP!" She stalked around her cell like a captured lion. Angry? She'd never felt so angry in her life! Hattie Quim had ruined her staff so bad, she had a good mind to sack them all on general principle.

Just you wait until I get out of here!
Absolute babel, that is!
"HELP!"

*

"So let us make it absolutely cleeeeeear!" sang the choir, dragging out the last note long enough for a toilet break and a trip to the concessions stand. "If it wasn't for Hattie, we wouldn't be here."

Cue applause.

It didn't come.

"Fucking choirs!"

BABY RUDOLPH

Cue Dorman, who did come, marching across the stage, clapping enough for everyone. With the microphone in one hand, it sounded like the opening to a New Order song.

"There we have it!" Dorman said as the choristers stepped down from the bleachers and filed out in a disorderly fashion. Hattie Quim turned, bowed, picked her crown up from the stage, bowed again. "What a... what a strange song choice," Dorman added. "But, I'm sure Ahora, had she been here, would have loved it." Of course, had Ahora been there, that nightmare would have never happened. It was almost enough to keep Schrödinger up at night.

The less said about the next performance, the better, so we'll keep it brief. Jessica Claus took to the stage, threw herself around a pole, and left again. The elflings in the audience, of course, had seen none of this, due to the parental hand in front of their eyes throughout the bit, but would later go home and find the routine online anyway, and after watching it, would give their parents a huge hug, say a family prayer, and promise to never disable the elfernet's parental controls again. The male elves spent the entire routine twiddling their thumbs and whistling; the female elves sat watching their husbands closely for any signs of erection, handbag in one hand and spouse's shirt collar in the other.

Everyone was glad when it was over and relaxed into their seats once again with a collective sigh.

As she came off the stage, Jessica rushed toward Finklefoot, who was preparing to take to the stage with his fellow *Bee Gees*, Jimbo and Rat. "I think I remember!" she said. "I saw him gawping at me from the front row and it jogged my memory!"

"Whoa, whoa," said Finklefoot. "Are you saying what I think you're saying?"

Jessica nodded. "I'm pretty sure," she said. "He's here, and worse than that, he's already performed—"

Out on the stage, Dorman had called out thrice for the *Bee Gees* and the audience were clapping wildly.

"Come on, Eff-eff!" Jimbo said, pulling Finklefoot by the collar, which had a second job as a beach windbreaker. "We're on!"

Finklefoot was pulled along by his friends toward Stage Left, where a fella with a clipboard was trying his best to look official. He scanned the piece of paper attached to the clipboard, ticked something off, then gave the threesome the nod.

Looking back, seeing Mrs. Claus standing there with her bits and bobs out, watching her nod and smile at him, and even give him a thumbs up, he knew they had done it. They had perhaps solved the mystery of Ahora's disappearance. Life could go back to normal, if what Jessica Claus knew was true. *Just get this pesky performance out of the way*, Finklefoot thought, *and then I'll find her, get the name, and all will be well.*

The audience cheered as three exceedingly small *Bee Gees* skipped onto the stage. Which one was Barry, Robin, or Maurice? It didn't matter in the slightest. Interchangeable, as a word, had been coined when the *Bee Gees* came onto the scene; before then there was just a blank spot in the dictionary between intercession and interchannel.

They started to sing, and to be fair to them—and you had to be, really, as they hadn't had any time to rehearse, not with everything going on—they sounded the part. And that part was that of slightly higher-pitched *Bee Gees*. They even *looked* the part, if you weren't looking too hard.

The medley went something like this: You Should be Dancing and Stayin' Alive, More Than a Woman and Too Much Heaven, slowing things down midway with How Deep Is Your Love? and Words, before cranking things up with Tragedy and culminating in Night Fever. It was fairly well-received, especially by the three people who had heard of the *Bee Gees*.

The trio accepted their applause gracefully and were on their second bow when Jimbo realised Finklefoot was no longer at the end of his arm.

Off to save the day, he thought, bowing one more time and leaving Stage Right in fits of jollity with his bandmate, Rat.

On the other side of the stage, Finklefoot searched the hubbub for Jessica, which shouldn't have been hard as she was a human amongst elves, likely to stick out like a sore thumb, but she wasn't there. She wasn't where she had been when he'd left her, which just goes to show, you can't leave them for five seconds without them deciding they had better things to be getting on with. The "them", of course, refers to *all* humans; you're not making a villain out of *this* otherworldly narrator.

"Fuck!" said Finklefoot and disappeared into the throng.

22

Rudolph had trotted on to the stage, snatched the mic from Dorman, and tore into his set before the audience realised they should have been clapping. Oh, well. He'd started now, and it would be rude to interrupt.

The jokes, like a premature ejaculator's convention, came thick and fast. Rudolph knew his timing was all wrong, and that he should have been giving them time to appreciate the nuance of his witticisms before moving on to the next, but he was not in the mood. He just wanted to get it over with so that he could return to his new life on the streets. He'd almost saved up enough money for a ham and cheese sandwich.

"I used to be addicted to the hokey cokey," said Rudolph, irritated, "but then I turned myself around. Why did the statue leave her husband? She was tired of being taken for granite. Why shouldn't you marry hardware engineers? They have floppy disks. My boss says I have a preoccupation with vengeance; we'll see about that." Like that, they relentlessly came for two minutes, and then three, and Rudolph was suddenly finding it increasingly difficult to breathe. He started to skip punchlines entirely, which isn't often seen on the comedy circuit because, as an idea, it defeats the point of a joke. That hadn't stopped Amy Schumer from building her career around it, but mostly, comedians pair their jokes with punchlines. The audience seems to prefer it that way. In other words, Rudolph had not only stepped off a well-trodden path, but he was also now skipping along in the bushes, kicking thistle and attracting grass adders.

"!"

Rudolph realised he had stopped talking completely, and that the room had fallen deathly silent. Someone at the side of the stage cleared their throat.

Rudolph stared into the lights.

The audience were there, somewhere in all that brightness; he could feel them, sitting anxiously, waiting for something to happen, wondering, *Is this part of the show, do you think?* because then, if it is, they can relax, knowing they're in the hooves of a consummate professional.

Rudolph waited, breathing deeply, listening to his own heartbeat.

Buddum... buddum... buddum...

Few heartbeats contain three dots, but Rudolph's did in that moment.

"Fucking choir!"

BABY RUDOLPH

"Not now, nobhead!"

Silence again.

Buddum... buddum...

"I can't do this," Rudolph said, quietly. A plaintive smile appeared on his face. "I can't do this anymore." He took a deep breath, stopped staring at the lights, and went to sit down on the stool in the middle of the stage. As he sat, he folded one hind leg over the other, made sure his lipstick wasn't out, and huffed into the microphone. "You know," he said, clearly in no rush, "I've been a comic for a while now, and the thing they don't tell you when you're starting out is this: when your audience isn't laughing, you die inside." Pause for dramatic effect. Audience still quieter than an amoeba's toot. Rudolph laughed ironically. "You'd think it'd be okay, that you'd be able to take those silences, that you've made them laugh before, you can do it again. But no, us comedians we take those quiet bits personally. Why aren't they still laughing? There should be no time to do anything else."

Buddum... buddum... buddum... Anyone would think a shark was about to crash through the stage and drag Rudolph, bloodied and screaming, into the depths below.

But they couldn't hear his beating heart, which rendered all that lovely imagery as pointless.

"I'm not an expert," Rudolph went on, since no one had had the temerity to pull him from the stage yet. Even in the wings they silently watched, because however this turned out, it would give them something to talk about later. Everyone loves a car crash; that's why rubberneckers always have whiplash. "I'm just trying to do my best," he said. "In everything. In life. In me. I'm trying to be the best me I can, and if I can be me, and no one calls me a cunt, then I'll know I'm doing something right at just being me, but the thing is…" A trailing off that would have won an Oscar, if there was a category for Suitable Ways to End a Sentence. "You never know you're being the real you until it's too late, you've already messed up or said something that's annoyed or hurt someone, and so now *that's* the real you… *that* person, who hurts people."

At the side of the stage, Jimbo asked, "Is any of this making sense to you?"

Finklefoot had given up on finding Jessica Claus and had returned to his bandmates. "Not in the slightest," he whispered back. "Is there a subplot we don't know about?"

BABY RUDOLPH

Rat squeezed between them. "Have you ever considered the fact that *you're* the subplot? You might be the filler in this one?"

Finklefoot frowned and adjusted his monocle. "Highly unlikely," he whispered.

"Yeah," agreed Jimbo. "Sounds far-fetched to me."

The drone camera marked Fourth Wall hovered in front of their still-thinking faces momentarily before zipping off to work on the next *Deadpool* movie.

"I've had a rough time lately," Rudolph said, because all that nonsense with the *Bee Gees* and the drone camera had been a sub-subplot. "Things have got bad, and I'm, well, I'm fucking homeless." A few whispers in the audience; a little, innocent voice said, *I know what those words mean, Mom, it means he likes shagging hobos.*

"I mean," Rudolph continued, because it was not his place to clobber someone else's elfling. "I *have* a home; I just can't get to it. It's still there, but so is *she*, and I'm scared." A tear, slow and steady, rolled down his cheek. "I'm scared of *her*, and so I'm sleeping in an alleyway next to a pizza place now. That's me, everyone's favourite magical reindeer, scavenging bins for crusts and bits of burnt mozzarella. All because I was nice to someone, and she does deserve it. No one should be treated the way she has, the way I once was, the way most of you have been at some point or other."

"He's really going on with this bit, don't you think?" said Jimbo.

"Probably hoping it gets snapped up by *Notflix.*" Finklefoot shook his head and looked at his watch, which had given up ages ago and was now stuck perpetually on half-three.

"There you are," said a treacly, seductive voice. "I've been looking for you."

Jessica Claus, now wearing a red satin gown with fluffy white trim, lowered herself to Finklefoot's ear and began to whisper.

"Oh!" he said. "Well, fuck me sideways!"

On the stage Rudolph's diatribe was becoming boring. A few beings had started to leave, the doors at the back squeaking noisily every time someone did.

"That's fine," Rudolph said, because he wasn't going to let anything as insubstantial as an obvious hint get in the way of a good ending. "You can all leave. I used to think I could, too, but you know what you can't leave? You know what you can never leave? *You.* You can never leave *you*, and that—"

BABY RUDOLPH

"Right, that's enough o' that bollocks, ya wee flap o' foreskin!"

The audience turned to see who had interrupted, saw who it was, then went, "Errgh," and collectively clucked their tongues.

Merthyr made her way to the centre aisle (oh, yes, there is one. Just forgot to mention it, that's all); the spotlight followed her, because the lighting technician—Barry from the Lego department—knew the rumblings of a potential fight when he saw them, and to be brutally honest, he was sick of the sight of Rudolph.

"Ya think yer tae good fur me?" Merthyr said, breathing as if she'd just challenged for first place in a triathlon. Of course, she had no idea what a triathlon was; to her, it was that special coating they put on frying pans to stop your omelette from sticking. "Ah offered ye th' world, babeh Rudy! Ah offered ye all of me!"

She dragged a hind hoof back on the floor, and again, and again, winding up to launch herself forward.

On the stage, Rudolph sat still, eyes wide, paralysed. His life flashed before him, which took some doing when you were around to send Jesus a first birthday card. The postal service was different back then. It had worked, for starters, so long as your carrier pigeon wasn't one of the unfortunates forced onto a bloody big boat with two of everything else.

"Sorry?" Rudolph whimpered. And, "I can't move."

Merthyr grinned. The audience went *ooh!* and watched as the reindeer with the pink cardigan and ridiculous perm took off at full pelt toward the stage.

"Ah!" managed Rudolph.

"He's fucked!" said Finklefoot.

"Look out!" an anthropomorphic owl added. No one had noticed that one, perched up high in the corner, but there he was. The owl couldn't look, so quickly turned its head fully around in that weird way they invariably do.

And then Merthyr was airborne, a huge, furry missile up near the lighting rig. "Ah fuckin' love ye, babeh Rudy!" she roared, and then came down toward the stage a lot quicker than she'd gone up. Rudolph silently screamed, and through peer pressure alone, the audience joined it.

That was when everything started to move in slow-motion, which makes it a lot easier to put into words, thank Santa! Because as Merthyr came down, destined to crush poor Rudolph where he sat motionless and with his eyes clenched shut, there came a noise that changed the course of events entirely.

BABY RUDOLPH

Grunt-whistle-thump-crash.

*

Ahora had been picking rat-meat from her teeth with a small bone when the roof crashed inwards. One minute it was up there, holding up the upstairs floor, the next it was on the ground. Fortunately, she was shielded from the wooden shrapnel on all sides by big metal bars, but it still came as a bit of a shock. I mean, if you can't trust ceilings, what can you trust?

After about thirty seconds, the dust began to settle, and Ahora was suddenly aware that there was a fat reindeer lying in the middle of the room with an arrow sticking out of its backside.

"Bastard! said the reindeer, but it made no attempt to move. It might have had something to do with all the wood it was buried under, not to mention the old Singer sewing machine on its head. "Ahm fairly sure a've broke mah back!"

"Ahora!" a voice from above said.

"God?" replied Ahora.

"No," said the voice. "Not God, Ahora. It's Finklefoot."

"Who?" She looked up at the massive hole where there had once been rafters and planks. There were about a dozen faces staring down into the hole. "Oh, it's *you*," she said, recognising Finklefoot immediately. "Should have known you were involved in all this." And she tisked. "Can someone get me out of this cell, please?" she said, surveying the damage. You would think that someone who made jigsaw puzzles for a living would be able to piece together what the hell was going on, but no. She hadn't a bloody clue.

"We'll have you out of there in a jiffy," Finklefoot said.

Three hours later...

*

Most of the audience had gone home, but a few stragglers had stuck around to see how it all turned out. Their reasoning was this: you don't walk out of a *Fast and Furious* movie just before the engines start. Also, many of them wanted to know how they were going to get that fat reindeer out of that hole. They hadn't been expecting a JCB and an industrial hoist to show up, but they did, and the reindeer was soon out of there and plonked on the stage like a gigantic scrotum.

BABY RUDOLPH

"Can someone get th' arrow oota mah arse?" said Merthyr Titful, pitifully. "Ahm pretty sure tis gaen all th' way through 'n' is touching mah fud."

Norm walked across to where she lay, snapped the arrow off halfway, and said, "You're lucky. I was aiming for your turd processor," before leaving Stage Left.

"Get that thing to the hospital," said Chief Quim to his only officer. "When she's feeling better, we'll arrange a fair trial, but I foresee a cell in her future."

"Ah!" said Finklefoot. This was hi*s Columbo* moment, and he was going to make sure it was done correctly, with gusto, and with his face to the audience, who still wouldn't go home. Fucking ghouls.

He had his cast of players right there with him on the stage, all except for—

"What's going on, then?" Ahora said, marching onto the stage from the right. Rather good she was, too. Like a young Hepburn. Or an old Garland. "Have you collared the bastard who's had me cooped up down there for the best part of a week?"

Ten of them, there were, just like that old book with the Indians and the island. The one by Agatha Crispy. There was Finklefoot and Jimbo, Hattie and Chief Quim, Officer

Dufflecoat and Jessica Claus, Rat and Rudolph, Merthyr and Shart, but he was unconscious in the corner, dreaming of sharp objects.

"Well," said Finklefoot knowingly. He had the audience on tenterhooks; the owl in the corner turned away again. He walked across the stage, disappeared behind the curtain, and came back carrying a Tesco's carrier bag. "This may come as a shock to you, Ahora, but I believe that your abductor is right here, in this very room."

"Well, bugger me!" said Ahora, clutching at her chest and scanning the audience for 'them wot done it'. She was *really* good. Like Judi Dench or Vin Diesel.

"Not only that," continued Finklefoot, switching his monocle to the other eye. It was starting to get a bit sore. He was considering switching to a different gimmick. A stammer, perhaps, or just one bollock. "I believe," he went on, "that your abductor is up here, standing on this very stage."

Ooh, went the audience.

"Hooo!" went the owl.

"No they're not," said Ahora, which fairly put the brakes on things.

"That's right, I—what do you *mean* they're not?"

BABY RUDOLPH

Ahora frowned and glanced about the stage. "Well, they're *not*," she said. "On this very stage." She walked up and down, giving each suspect a modicum of scrutiny, and when she was satisfied she was telling the truth, she said, "Nope. I'd recognise that little devil anywhere!"

Not to be perturbed—the good bit was coming up, if he could only hold his own water for a few seconds more—Finklefoot began to riffle through the carrier bag, and came out with two things: a giant, permed wig and a pink cardigan.

Ahora visibly recoiled at the appearance of these props.

"Someone has good taste," Merthyr grumbled from the floor.

"These," Finklefoot said, "were found at the top of the stairs leading into the trap room. Easy for our elfnapper to put them on and take them off as they came and went. A disguise that... well, if I'm being honest, it's not the greatest disguise in the world."

"It's the whole Superman's spectacles thing again," Jimbo said. "The disguise works because, well, no one believes that Clark Kent could ever be Superman. It's about character. How could a bumbling reporter from Smallville be Superman? Sure, they look exactly the same, but no, not a chance because Superman can fly and, well, Clark can't. Not only that but he's always falling down open manholes, banging into things, hitting his thumb with hammers, stubbing his toes on recalcitrant furniture. Superman would *never* do those things, so to even *consider* the truth, that Clark and Superman are one and the same, is ridiculous. Clark Kent could turn up to a fancy dress party wearing the cape and the boots and his pants on the outside, and no one would bat an eye."

"So, what you're saying, in a rather protracted way," said Hattie Quim, "is that she wouldn't recognise her abductor unless they had their wig on."

Jimbo nodded. "Because they, whoever they are, couldn't *possibly* be the elfnapper. Perish the thought."

"Yes, well," said Finklefoot, "I was going to get to all that later on, but you've saved me a job."

"Who is it, then?" queried Hattie Quim.

Finklefoot smiled and walked slowly across to where Hattie stood beside her husband. He plonked the wig down on Chief Quim's head, elfhandled him into the pink cardigan, took a step back and turned to Ahora, who slapped a hand to her mouth in complete shock.

BABY RUDOLPH

"That's her!" Ahora gasped. "That's her there!" She pointed an accusatory finger at the bewigged Chief of Police, who was taking it all in his stride.

Fair cop, guv'nor, I know I has done wrong. I'll come quietly.

Chief Quim turned to face his wife, who looked like she'd just seen a ghost... and then the ghost had touched her inappropriately.

"No," said Hattie. "Please tell me she's—"

"I did it for *you*, Hattie," Chief Quim said. "I know how much it meant to you, leading that choir today, and the jigsaw factory has all the best singers. I had to take Ahora out of the mix for a little while, just until you realised your dream." He looked down at the ground, at his highly-polished, standard-police-issued elf shoes, and shook his head. "I did it for *you*, Hattie," he said, and then to everyone on the stage, he added, "I did it for my wife."

As moments went it was, well, it was certainly one of them.

"Just out of curiosity," said Chief Quim to Finklefoot, "how did you know it was me?"

"Ah, I'm so glad you asked," Finklefoot replied. "You see, at the scene of the abduction we found a chloroformed hankie and this!" He produced the Carmex Classic Cherry and Strawberry lip-balm and held it up like he was auditioning for *The Lion King*. When no one reacted, he put his arm down and went on. "My associate and I of FF&J Investigations figured out that, since elves don't have fingerprints, or indeed, lip prints, we approached that woman there," he nodded in the direction of Jessica Claus, who pinched her nipples and moaned in reply, "who is an expert in elf lips. Specifically, those of the male persuasion. So—"

"Never mind!" said Chief Quim, looking nervously at his wife, who was currently in the process of putting two and two together and coming up with infidelity. "I'll just cuff myself and be off to the station."

"Fucking choir!" that elf shouted again.

Finklefoot smiled, walked to the centre-front of the stage, and took a bow. His monocle fell off and rolled somewhere into the empty front row. There was no applause this time, but there *was* a shuffling of tiny feet as the stragglers made for the exit, and there *was* the squeaking of that bloody door as they proceeded to leave through it.

"That was a bit of a cop out," one elf said.

BABY RUDOLPH

"I've never been *deus ex machina*'d so hard in my life," said another. "And that wig was a MacGuffin, an' all!"

23

Rudolph woke up in his own bedding, in his own stable, stretched and yawned and slapped his lips. Outside, the birds were singing their beautiful songs; a little, chirpy voice belonging to a chaffinch choirmaster said, "That's just glorious! Keep it up! And let's give it some welly!"

After taking his morning piss, Rudolph checked his *MyFace*, saw that his inbox was empty, and declared that to be a good thing.

He sighed contentedly and left his stable by the front door, something he would have to get used to again, but it was getting easier each day. *Pretty soon*, he thought, *I'll be able to sleep with both eyes closed.*

No one followed him to the practice rinks that day, or ever again.

*

"Three pints of 'same again'," said Finklefoot, counting out loose change and hoping he had enough. If not, Rat could pay for his own, since he hadn't contributed much to the plot. It was the least he could do. Finklefoot needn't have worried, though, as Norm chucked the coins in the till and slammed it shut without even counting them.

"You know," Finklefoot said to Norm, who was pouring their drinks, "you shouldn't be so trusting, Norm."

"What?"

"I said," repeated Finklefoot, "that you should be careful who you put your trust in. I mean, I could have just paid for those drinks with chocolate coins, pfennigs, or expired drachma, but you didn't even check, you just put them in your till."

"Did you pay me in pfennigs and expired drachma?" Norm said, pouring the second of three pints. He didn't even look up. Took his pint pouring very seriously, did Norm. One tiny over-pour and he'd have to start all over again.

Finklefoot exchange a look with Jimbo; Rat was too busy hustling someone on the pool table to take part. Two extras in the background said, "Rhubarb, rhubarb, rhubarb," but without making too much noise about it.

"No," said Finklefoot. "I didn't. I'm just saying that I *could* have."

"No you couldn't," said Norm. "I'll hunt you down with my bow if you do, and you don't want that, no one wants that, so you couldn't pay me in dodgy currency, *could* you?" He pushed, with great effort, three pints across the sticky bar. "Not if you know what's good for you."

Finklefoot scraped the froth from his pint with a dirty beer-mat and said, "Well, I guess there are certain things and certain people we *can* still trust, after all." Mainly because he didn't want an arrow in the arse.

"To us!" he said, holding his pint up.

"To us!" Jimbo said, clinking glasses. "And to FF&J Investigations. Long may be solve those mysteries that no one else will touch with a bargepole."

The doors to *The Partridge Inn* suddenly flew open, and three men dressed in expensive suits came through them, carrying briefcases and an air of superiority. You could say what you wanted about the plot, but the budget had been put to good use.

The man in the middle—there's always one in the middle, Finklefoot thought suspiciously. Especially when there's three of them—set his briefcase down on the bar and addressed Norm with, "We're looking for Finklefoot, Jimbo, Rat, and Norm." He opened the case with a combination—

BABY RUDOLPH

1234, Finklefoot noticed—and drew from it several pieces of paper and a rather expensive-looking pen.

"I'm Norm," said Norm, which was roughly the correct answer, "and these fellas here are Finklefoot and Jimbo."

"Someone say my name?" said Rat, appearing at the bar with a pool cue in one hand and a cheese and onion cob in the other.

"You must be Rat," said the main man, the one with the speaking role. He hadn't fluffed any of his lines so far, which bode well for his future.

"What's this all about?" Finklefoot asked, then necked half his 'same again' and wiped his beard on his sleeve. "If it's anything to do with tax, I'm afraid you're barking up the wrong tree. We're exempt, you see, on account of not wanting to pay any."

The suited man laughed. The two non-speaking suits behind him joined in. Not too much, though; just enough to ensure they featured in the cut version.

"We are from *Notflix*," said the one in the middle. "I'm Bob, this is Bob, and that one there is Bob."

"I'll never remember all that," said Jimbo.

BABY RUDOLPH

This all seems a little... insensitive. A bit exploitative. A little too close to home, if you know what I mean."

"Yeah, Jimbo's right," said Finklefoot. "I mean, how do you think Rudolph's going to feel, having to live his ordeal all over again and again?"

"Rudolph's already on board," said Bob. "As long as he gets to play himself, and the special effects team does a good job on the giant Merthyr puppet, he's all-in."

Finklefoot and Jimbo exchanged a look.

"How come I never get a look?" said Rat.

"Not now, Rat," said Finklefoot. "We're thinking."

Bob, the one in the middle said, "Maybe this might help with your decision," and he removed four little pieces of paper from the briefcase and handed them out accordingly.

Checks, they were. Or *cheques*, if you prefer. We're all God's creatures, after all.

"Never in my life," said Finklefoot with a tremulous voice, "have I seen so many zeroes in the same place at once."

Rat looked at his own check and said, "There's only one zero on mine." He grinned. "That's awesome! Fifty buckaroos for doing absolutely nothing!"

For the final time that day, Finklefoot and Jimbo shared a look, and then they turned to Bob, Bob, and Bob and said:

"We're here to make you an offer for your story," he said, then one of the Bobs behind him gave him a surreptitious kick, and he said, "Sub-story. I meant your sub-story."

"I'm confused," said Norm. "Is this a sexual thing?"

The Bobs assured all four of them that this was real, and definitely nothing sexual at all. What it all boiled down to was this: Bob, Bob and Bob wanted the rights to their side of events for what had happened the past week. There was most certainly a market for a story like this, and if viewing figures were good after Season One, they could make something up to drag it out for further series, perhaps *ad nauseum*.

"People *watch* shit like that?" said Finklefoot, dubious.

"Oh, yes!" said Bob. Which one, it didn't matter. "People will watch any old shit, so long as we put BASED ON A TRUE STORY at the start. They've usually switched it off by the time the credits roll, and the disclaimer at the end says, WHILE SITUATIONS AND PEOPLE WERE LOOSELY BASED ON TRUE EVENTS, WE DID TAKE CERTAIN LIBERTIES AND FIDDLED WITH THINGS, CHARACTERS, PLACES, AND ALL THE REST OF IT, FOR ENTERTAINMENT PURPOSES."

"I'm not sure about this," said Jimbo. "I mean, I heard about all that stuff with Rudolph and that Merthyr creature.

"Where do we sign?"

*

BABY RUDOLPH WENT ON TO BECOME THE MOST-STREAMED NOTFLIX SHOW OF ALL TIME, AND WON ELFIES ACROSS THE BOARD FOR BEST ACTOR, BEST SUPPORTING ACTOR, BEST SET DESIGN, BEST CATERING, AND BEST USE OF PUPPETEERING IN A LIMITED SERIES.

MERTHYR TITFUL COMPLETED A TWELVE-MONTH ANGER MANAGEMENT COURSE AND IS CURRENTLY WORKING AS A SOCIAL MEDIA MANAGER, WHERE SHE CAN FOLLOW AS MANY PEOPLE AS SHE WANTS WITHOUT REPERCUSSION.

CHIEF QUIM OF THE LCPD WAS DEMOTED TO OFFICER AND GIVEN AN EIGHTEEN-MONTH SUSPENDED SENTENCE AND THREE POINTS ON HIS SNOW-SKI LICENSE JUST FOR FUN.

OFFICER DUFFLECOAT WAS PROMOTED TO CHIEF OF POLICE. HE STILL WEARS A DEERSTALKER AND SMOKES A CALABASH, BECAUSE ONCE A DICKHEAD, ALWAYS A DICKHEAD.

BABY RUDOLPH

FF&J INVESTIGATIONS CONTINUES TO OPERATE, BETWEEN SHIFTS AT THE TOY FACTORY AND WHEN THEIR WIVES SAY SO. ALL THOSE ZEROES ON THOSE CHECKS QUICKLY DWINDLED, BUT IN FINKLEFOOT'S WORDS, "WHO NEEDS MONEY WHEN YOU'VE GOT GOOD FRIENDS AND FAMILY?" HE CONTINUES TO LIE TO THIS DAY.

JESSICA CLAUS IS STILL INTO LITTLE PEOPLE. BUT MOST OF THE TIME, THEY ARE INTO HER.

THE FAT BASTARD REMAINS BLISSFULLY UNAWARE OF MOST THINGS, BUT FINALLY HAS HIS PAPERWORK IN ORDER.

THE END